SCHOLASTIC

Practice, Practice, Practice!

WORD PROBLEMS

by Judith A. Muschla
and
Gary Robert Muschla

New York • Toronto • London • Auckland • Sydney
Mexico City • New Delhi • Hong Kong • Buenos Aires

Teaching
Resources

Dedication

For Erin

Cover design by Maria Lilja

Interior design by Ellen Matlach for Boultinghouse & Boultinghouse, Inc.

Interior illustrations by Teresa Anderko

ISBN: 0-439-52963-8

9 10   40   13

Contents

Introduction

The skills necessary for solving word problems are among the most demanding and important students must master. Along with a fundamental understanding of mathematical facts and processes, solving word problems requires critical thinking, decision making, and the use of multiple operations. More than other types of problems, word problems can reflect real-life situations that illustrate the value of mathematics to everyday living.

We have three major objectives for writing *Practice, Practice, Practice! Word Problems:*

- To provide students with skills-based reproducible worksheets containing word problems that will help them to master the skills found in the typical fourth- through eighth-grade mathematics curriculum.

- To provide students with activities that adhere to the Principles and Standards of the NCTM and that promote the mastery of higher-level problem-solving skills.

- To provide students with word problems that are motivating, challenging, and fun.

What This Book Contains

This book contains 50 reproducible worksheets of word problems that address the skills found in the typical fourth- through eighth-grade mathematics curriculum. The worksheets, which cover a broad range of skills, progress from basic to challenging, and require students to use a variety of problem-solving strategies.

Each worksheet is built around a central concept or real-life situation with which students can identify. This stimulates interest, as well as helps students to understand the background and vocabulary of the problems. The worksheets generally contain between 6 and 12 questions appearing in 5 to 7 problems. Many of the problems have multiple steps. The last problem of most of the worksheets is a "think piece" that is opened-ended and requires students to write an explanation of their answer. Students can write their explanations on the back of the worksheet or on a separate sheet of paper.

An answer key is included at the end of the book. For problems in which answers may vary or that need explanations, possible answers are offered.

How to Use This Book

Each worksheet in this book stands alone and may be used in the manner that best satisfies the needs of your students. You may use the worksheets in various ways: to supplement your instruction, for reinforcement, for extra credit, for challenges, or for substitute plans.

The worksheets are designed for easy implementation. Each is reproducible, has a basic level of readability, and requires no additional materials. You may encourage students to use calculators for computation, or you may instruct them to work the problems out for practice and for enhancing number sense.

While the titles of the worksheets are related to the material on which the problems are based, each worksheet is also labeled with the skill, or skills, the problems address. These skills are also included in the table of contents beneath the title of the worksheet. Thus, the contents functions as a skills list, making it easy for you to identify those worksheets that will be of most benefit to your students.

To help your students with their problem-solving efforts, you may wish to distribute copies of "Strategies for Solving Word Problems," on page 7. Discuss the strategies with your students and encourage them to employ the suggestions as they solve word problems.

Connections to the NCTM Principles and Standards

All of the worksheets in this book align with the NCTM's Principles and Standards for School Mathematics. Along with problem-solving skills, the material in this book fosters the development of proficiency in computation, estimation, and mathematical reasoning.

We trust that your students will find the problems on these worksheets interesting and enjoyable, and that you will find this book to be a welcomed addition to your math program. We wish you well with your teaching.

Judith A. Muschla
Gary Robert Muschla

Strategies for Solving Word Problems

Most word problems are easier to solve if you follow these suggestions:

- **Read the problem carefully and concentrate** on what it is asking. You may find that you have to read the problem two or three times or more.

- **Understand the problem.** Make sure you understand the information provided and what the problem wants you to find. Decide what information is needed to solve the problem (some problems may contain too much or too little information). Also
  - Use your imagination to "see" what is happening in the problem.
  - Draw a picture to help you find relationships.
  - Look for patterns.
  - View the problem from different angles.
  - Make a table or drawing.

- **Decide on a plan for solving the problem.** What operation, or operations, are needed? Also
  - Use guess and check to find possible solutions.
  - Try to make the problem simpler. For example, for problems with fractions or decimals, substitute whole numbers to help you recognize what operations are needed.
  - Write an equation.
  - Estimate possible answers.
  - Try to work backward.

- **Solve the problem.** Double-check your math.

- **Consider your answer.** Does it make sense? Did you answer the question that was asked?

Body Facts

The human body is far more complicated than the most advanced machine. Use the body facts below to solve the problems.

1 The average baby's body has 350 bones. As a person gets older, some of these bones grow together. This is why the average adult has 206 bones. What is the difference between the number of bones in the body of the average adult and the body of the average baby?

_____

2 Doctors recommend that the average person should exercise at least 30 minutes every day. How many minutes of exercise is this each week?

_____

How many hours of exercise is this each week?

_____

3 The average person has 650 muscles. Fourteen muscles are needed for smiling, but 43 muscles are needed for frowning. How many muscles are not needed for frowning?

_____

4 The average person breathes 20 times per minute during normal activity. Based on this rate, how many breaths does the average person take each hour?

Each day? _____

5 The average person's heart beats 100,000 times per day. How many beats is this per hour? (Round answers to the nearest whole number.)

_____

How many beats is this per minute?

_____

6 Jim works out every day in hopes of making his school's football team. His doctor suggests that he eat between 2,800 and 2,900 calories per day. He also encourages Jim to eat a balanced diet.

For breakfast and lunch, Jim has eaten 1,475 calories. For dinner he has a choice of the following foods:

- hamburger with bun (420 calories)
- baked potato with butter (190 calories)
- small salad with dressing (155 calories)
- glass of low-fat milk (200 calories)
- piece of apple pie (395 calories)
- bottle of spring water (0 calories)

Jim can have up to three servings of each food. What foods, and how many servings of each, should Jim choose to reach his goal of eating between 2,800 and 2,900 calories? How many calories will these choices give him? Explain why you chose these foods. Write your answers on the back of this page.

Name _____   Date _____

Highs and Lows

Becky has always been interested in geography. Recently she learned that the surface of Earth varies miles in elevation. Solve the following problems about the highs and lows of Earth's surface.

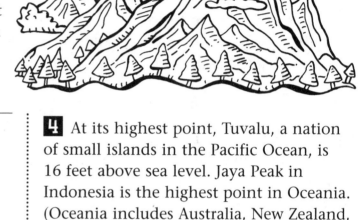

1 At 29,035 feet in elevation, Mt. Everest in Tibet/Nepal is the highest mountain in the world. The next highest mountain is Mt. Aconcagua in Argentina at 22,834 feet. How much taller is Mt. Everest than Mt. Aconcagua?

2 Mt. Pico of the Azores Islands is the world's tallest underwater mountain. It rises 20,000 feet from the ocean floor to the surface. It rises another 7,711 feet above the ocean surface. Mt. McKinley is the highest mountain in North America, with an elevation 20,320 feet. How much taller is Mt. Pico than Mt. McKinley?

3 The Marianas Trench in the Pacific Ocean contains the deepest part of any ocean, at 36,198 feet. What is the distance in feet between the deepest part of the Marianas Trench and the peak of Mt. Everest (29,035 feet)?

A mile equals 5,280 feet. About how many miles is the distance between the lowest part of the Marianas Trench and the peak of Mt. Everest? (Round your answer to the nearest mile.)

4 At its highest point, Tuvalu, a nation of small islands in the Pacific Ocean, is 16 feet above sea level. Jaya Peak in Indonesia is the highest point in Oceania. (Oceania includes Australia, New Zealand, and the Pacific Islands.) If Jaya Peak is about 1,030 times the highest elevation of Tuvalu, what is the approximate elevation of Jaya Peak?

The exact elevation of Jaya Peak is 16,500 feet. What is the difference between your approximate elevation and the exact elevation?

5 The Dead Sea in Israel/Jordan averages 1,349 feet below sea level. The Caspian Sea in Russia averages 92 feet below sea level. About how many more times below sea level is the Dead Sea than the Caspian Sea? (Round your answer to the nearest whole number.)

Name _____   Date _____

Taryn's Fractions

Fractions play an important part in Taryn's life. Solve the following problems. Simplify your answers.

1 Last week Taryn jogged $2\frac{1}{2}$ miles on Monday, $3\frac{3}{4}$ miles on Wednesday, and $2\frac{3}{8}$ miles on Saturday. How far did she jog in all last week?

_____

2 Aunt Inez's recipe for punch called for $4\frac{1}{2}$ quarts of apple cider. When Taryn decided to make her aunt's punch, she had only $3\frac{2}{3}$ quarts of cider. How much more did she need?

_____

3 Taryn tries to volunteer 6 hours each week at the animal shelter. Last week she worked $1\frac{1}{2}$ hours at the shelter on Tuesday and $3\frac{3}{4}$ hours on Thursday. By how much did she fall short of her goal last week?

_____

4 Taryn's mother drives $25\frac{3}{4}$ miles to work each day. Her father drives $18\frac{5}{6}$ miles. Assuming they take the same roads home that they take to work, how much farther is Taryn's mother's round-trip drive than her father's?

_____

5 Sal and Taryn grew bean plants for a science experiment. At the beginning of the month, Sal's plant was $3\frac{1}{4}$ inches tall and Taryn's was $2\frac{1}{4}$ inches tall. Two weeks later, Sal's plant was $4\frac{1}{2}$ inches tall and Taryn's was $3\frac{7}{8}$ inches tall. Whose plant grew more during that two-week period?

_____

By how much?

_____

6 Taryn estimated that she found about $\frac{1}{4}$ of the information she needed for her science report in reference books in school, $\frac{1}{2}$ from sources on the Internet, and $\frac{1}{3}$ from books at the public library. Are her estimates reasonable? Explain.

_____

_____

_____

_____

_____

_____

_____

Name _____ Date _____

Harris Middle School

Fractions are used at Harris Middle School in many ways. Solve the problems. Simplify your answers.

1 Rondel has 27 math problems to do for homework. If he finishes $\frac{1}{3}$ them before dinner, how many problems must he do after dinner?

_____

2 For the school play, Mr. Simmons helped students build the background for the stage. One background required that he cut a 16-foot board into $1\frac{1}{3}$-foot pieces. How many pieces did he cut?

_____

3 Jess spent $1\frac{1}{2}$ hours on the Internet. She spent $\frac{4}{5}$ of this time researching for her history report and the rest of the time surfing the Net. How many minutes did she surf the Net?

_____

4 There are 120 students in the Harris Middle School Band. If $\frac{1}{5}$ play string instruments, how many students play string instruments?

_____

If another $\frac{2}{5}$ play brass instruments, how many play brass instruments?

_____

If $\frac{1}{3}$ play woodwinds, how many play woodwinds?

_____

Of those playing woodwinds, 15 play the clarinet. Write a simplified fraction representing the number of students who play clarinet compared to the overall number of students who play woodwinds.

_____

5 Mrs. Walford, the art teacher at Harris Middle School, plans to make holiday decorations with her 7th period class. She has a $32\frac{1}{2}$-foot roll of green ribbon. Each decoration requires a $1\frac{3}{4}$ foot-long ribbon. How many decorations can she make?

_____

Mrs. Walford's class has 24 students, and there will be one decoration for each student. How much more ribbon will she need? (She cannot use the leftover ribbon from the previous roll.)

_____

6 The PTA donated 720 tulip bulbs to be planted around the school. $\frac{1}{4}$ of the total would be planted in flower beds around the school's front sign, $\frac{1}{3}$ would be planted on the sides of the school, and $\frac{2}{5}$ would be planted in the school's courtyard. This would leave 30 tulips for planting in other places. Is this an accurate plan? Explain your answer on the back of this page.

12

Dan's Ski Trip

Dan and three of his friends went skiing. Not only did they learn how to ski, but they learned about fractions, too. Solve the problems. Simplify your answers.

1 Dan's second run down Pine Tree Slope was $1\frac{1}{2}$ minutes faster than his first run. If his first run took $6\frac{3}{4}$ minutes, what was the time of his second run?

_____

2 Rocky Mount Trail is $1\frac{2}{3}$ miles long. If Dan skied this trail three times, how far did he ski?

_____

3 In the morning, Dan skied a total distance of $7\frac{3}{10}$ miles. In the afternoon, he skied a total distance of $6\frac{1}{4}$ miles. Dan's friend Marcus skied a total of $13\frac{1}{2}$ miles all day. Who skied farther?

_____

By how much?

_____

4 Dan and his three friends ate lunch at the ski lodge. They bought $1\frac{1}{2}$ pizzas and a 6-pint pitcher of juice. A whole pizza is cut into 8 pieces. Assuming Dan and each of his friends eat an equal number of slices, how many pieces of pizza did each eat?

_____

If the glasses for their juice each held $\frac{3}{4}$ pint, how many servings were in the 6-pint pitcher?

_____

5 Dan's friends Vince and Antonio went cross-country skiing. They skied $7\frac{4}{5}$ miles in 3 hours. How far did they travel each hour?

_____

6 The next time Dan went skiing, he skied Pine Tree Slope, which was $1\frac{3}{4}$ miles, two times; Rocky Mount Trail, $1\frac{2}{3}$ miles, three times; and Devil's Run, $2\frac{3}{8}$ miles, once. He estimated that he skied a total of 12 miles this day. Is his estimate valid? Explain.

_____

_____

_____

_____

_____

_____

_____

Name _____ Date _____

Uncle Al's Bakery

Danielle works in Uncle Al's bakery every Saturday. She has found that understanding fractions helps her with her work. Solve the problems. Simplify all answers.

1 Uncle Al baked brownies in a rectangular pan. He cut the brownies into 72 equal pieces and offered them as samples to his customers. By 9 A.M., $\frac{3}{4}$ of the brownies had been eaten. How many brownies were left?

_____

2 Uncle Al asked Danielle to package 48 chocolate chip cookies. She wrapped $\frac{2}{3}$ of them in the morning and then went to lunch. How many cookies did she have to wrap when she returned?

_____

3 To make his special apple turnovers, Uncle Al used $7\frac{1}{4}$ cups of apples. To make his special apple pie, he used $5\frac{1}{2}$ cups of apples. How many cups of apples did he use in all?

_____

4 Uncle Al's recipe for pumpkin bread requires $2\frac{1}{4}$ cups of pumpkin. He has 12 cups of pumpkin. How many complete loaves of pumpkin bread can he bake?

_____

How much pumpkin is left over?

_____

How much more pumpkin does he need to make one more loaf of pumpkin bread?

_____

5 When the bakery opened, Uncle Al had 120 oatmeal cookies. He sold $\frac{1}{3}$ of the total in the morning and $\frac{1}{2}$ in the afternoon. How many oatmeal cookies were left at the end of the day?

_____

6 A biscuit recipe requires $1\frac{3}{4}$ cups of biscuit mix and $\frac{3}{4}$ cup of Uncle Al's secret biscuit ingredient. These amounts will make two biscuits. Uncle Al asked Danielle to prepare enough mix for a dozen biscuits. How much biscuit mix and how much of the secret ingredient will she need?

_____

7 Uncle Al's recipe for cupcakes calls for making 24 dozen. After selling $\frac{7}{8}$ of the cupcakes, he got an order for 4 dozen more. Did he have enough cupcakes to fill the order? Explain.

_____

_____

_____

Practice, Practice, Practice! Word Problems Scholastic Teaching Resources

Track Team Decimals

Until he joined his school's track team, Darrin did not realize how important decimals were to track and field. Solve the problems.

1 Yesterday Darrin started track practice after school at 3 P.M. Practice lasted 2.25 hours. What time did practice end?

_____

2 Darrin practiced the following amounts of time last week: Monday, 2.5 hours; Tuesday, 2.25 hours; Wednesday, 0.75 hour; Thursday, 1 hour; and Friday, 2 hours. How long did he practice last week?

_____

3 Darrin runs the hundred-meter dash. In his first three runs yesterday, his times were 14.2 seconds, 13.84 seconds, and 13.63 seconds. How much faster was his second run than his first run?

_____

How much faster was his best run than his slowest run?

_____

4 Darrin's best time in the hundred-meter dash this season is 13.25 seconds. At the beginning of the season, Darrin's first run in the hundred-meter dash was 14.51 seconds. How much did his time improve in the hundred-meter dash?

_____

Kendall's best time in the hundred-meter dash is 13.53 seconds. How much slower is Kendall's best time than Darrin's best time?

_____

5 Last Saturday and Sunday, there was no practice for the track team. To keep in shape, Darrin and Kendall jogged. On Saturday, Darrin jogged 3.5 miles, and on Sunday he jogged 3.75 miles. Kendall jogged 4 miles on Saturday and 2.7 miles on Sunday. Who jogged farther?

_____

By how much?

_____

6 Darrin's goal is to beat 13 seconds for the hundred-meter dash this season. When he started the season, his best time was 14.51 seconds. Each week for the past 6 weeks, he has improved his best time by an average of 0.21 second. If 10 days remain in the track season, is it likely he will break the 13-second mark for his best time? Explain.

_____

_____

_____

15

Name _____ Date _____

David and Decimals

To help his class understand the importance of decimals, David's teacher suggested that the students keep track of how often they used decimals each day. Solve the following problems that show how often David uses his understanding of decimals.

1 David and his father belong to a bicycle club. On Saturday they rode 25.2 kilometers in 3.5 hours. How many kilometers did they average per hour?

_____

2 David works part-time in a local hobby shop. Last week he worked 9.5 hours and was paid $69.35. How much did he earn each hour?

_____

3 As a member of his school's Student Council Activities Committee, David helped sell tickets for the winter play. Each ticket cost $2.75. If a total of 332 tickets were sold, how much money was collected?

_____

4 Last night it snowed 5.6 inches in David's town. This was the first snowfall of the season. If the average annual amount of snowfall in David's town is 7.5 times this amount, how many inches of snow can David expect this winter?

_____

Write a decimal to express this amount in feet.

_____

5 When David and his family visited his grandmother recently, they drove 261 miles round-trip. The drive to his grandmother's house took 2 hours and 30 minutes, or 2.5 hours. What was their average speed in miles per hour?

_____

They drove home on the same roads but encountered a lot of traffic. If their average speed on the return trip was 45 miles per hour, how long did they drive?

_____

How many hours and minutes was this?

_____

6 David and Neil both solved this math problem to find a mystery number: The mystery number is 2.25 times the quotient of 10 and 2.5. Unfortunately, the boys got different answers. David got 9 and Neil got 0.5625. Each boy double-checked his work and is convinced he is right. Which boy, if either, is correct? Explain any mistakes.

_____

_____

_____

Name _____   Date _____

Weather Extremes

Heather enjoys studying weather. She was surprised to learn how much the weather varies around the world. Use the following facts to solve the problems.

1 Arica, Chile, is one of the driest places on Earth, averaging 0.03 inch of rainfall a year. Buenaventura, Colombia, is one of the wettest. It averages 8,849 times as much rain a year as Arica. How much rain does Buenaventura receive in an average year?

_____

On July 4, 1956, it rained 1.23 inches in Unionville, Maryland, in one minute. How many times more is this than the average annual rainfall for Arica?

_____

2 Quillayute, Washington, is one of the wettest cities in the United States, averaging 105.18 inches of rainfall a year. Yuma, Arizona, is one of the driest cities in the U.S., averaging 3.17 inches of rainfall yearly. How much more rainfall does Quillayute receive than Yuma in an average year?

_____

How many feet of rainfall does Quillayute receive on average each year?

_____

Round the amount of rainfall Yuma receives in inches to the nearest inch.

_____

Write a decimal showing what part of a foot this amount represents.

_____

3 One of the largest 24-hour snowfalls in the U.S. occurred on April 14–15, 1921, in Silver Lake, Colorado, when it snowed 75.8 inches. Assuming the storm lasted a full day, what was the rate of snowfall per hour? (Round your answer to the nearest hundredth.)

_____

4 Christy's science project required her to record the daily high temperature in her town during the second week of February. She was then to calculate the average high temperature for these days. These were the high temperatures (in Fahrenheit):

Sun.	Mon.	Tues.	Wed.	Thur.	Fri.	Sat.
40.35°	42.5°	41°	44.8°	36.25°	37.6°	39.35°

Christy forgot to record the temperatures for Thursday, Friday, and Saturday, and she averaged the high temperatures of only the first four days of the week. She told Heather that her average was accurate, even though she did not include all of the data. Heather disagreed. Who was right? Explain your answer on the back of this page.

17

Name _____   Date _____

Camp Challenge

Ricky attended Camp Challenge this past summer, where his understanding of decimals proved to be very useful. Solve the following problems.

1 Each day the campers swam in Lake Challenge. The temperature of the lake's water was 65.35°F. Some campers found this to be chilly, because a person's normal body temperature is 98.6°F. How much colder was the lake's temperature than a normal body temperature?

_____

2 Last year, Ricky's town sponsored a bicycle marathon with the proceeds going to charity. The length of the course was 7.8 kilometers. The bicycle marathon at Camp Challenge was 2.25 times as long. How long was the course for the bicycle marathon at the camp?

_____

3 Ricky and several other campers participated in a 10.85-kilometer hike. They completed the hike in 3.5 hours. How many kilometers did they average per hour?

_____

4 The first time Ricky climbed the rock wall, he managed to reach a height of 15.75 feet. The top of the wall was 21 feet. How much farther did Ricky need to climb to reach the top?

_____

On his second attempt, he climbed 18.5 feet, but on his third try he slipped at 13.3 feet. What was the average height of his three climbs?

_____

How much more was his highest climb than his average?

_____

5 The obstacle course at camp was a true challenge. A camper had to climb a barricade, crawl through a tunnel, swing across a creek on a rope, jump over a low hedge, and sprint 100 yards to the finish. To prepare for the course, Ricky practiced each obstacle separately. (He did not run the complete course during practice.) His best time for each obstacle follows:

- barricade: 3.5 seconds
- tunnel: 5.85 seconds
- rope swing: 4.6 seconds
- hedge jump: 2.08 seconds
- sprint: 13.47 seconds

Based on these times, he is confident that he can finish the obstacle course in less than 30 seconds. Do you think Ricky's reasoning is sound? Explain your answer on the back of this page.

Practice, Practice, Practice! Word Problems   Scholastic Teaching Resources

Name _____   Date _____

The Class Trip

Veronica is a member of the seventh-grade Class Trip Committee in her school. It is the responsibility of the committee to organize fund-raisers to help pay for the class trip. Solve the following problems.

1 For the first fund-raiser, the Class Trip Committee organized a car wash. Student volunteers would wash a car for $2.75. Since students could use the school's water and parking lot, their only costs were for sponges, towels, and detergent. These totaled $48.89. Veronica and other volunteers washed 29 cars. After their costs for materials, how much money did they raise for the trip?

_____

2 During their school's readathon, the Class Trip Committee sponsored a book sale. Parents, students, and friends donated used books that the committee could sell. Paperback books were sold for $0.15 each and hardcover books were sold for $0.50 each. At the end of the day, Veronica tallied the number of books sold: 329 paperbacks and 163 hardcover books. How much did the committee earn from the sales of used books?

_____

3 In early spring, the committee organized a cookie sale. Parent volunteers baked 58 dozen cookies to be sold at the school during parent/teacher conferences. Each cookie cost $0.25. If all but 39 cookies were sold, how much money did the committee earn?

_____

4 For Mother's Day, the committee organized a flower sale. Three local nurseries donated the flowers, allowing the committee to keep all of the profits from the sale of the flowers. Geraniums were sold for $0.99 each. If the committee sold $121.77 worth of geraniums, how many geraniums did they sell?

_____

5 The final fund-raiser for the year is a school dance. The only costs for the dance are $300 for the DJ and $150 for security. Veronica and the other committee members estimate that 260 students will attend the dance. The committee would like to make at least a $200 profit on the dance. However, they know that if the price of tickets is too high, fewer students will attend the dance. What is the least amount they can charge for each ticket and still earn $200?

_____

Some members of the committee argue that they should sell tickets for $3.00 each. Veronica believes that this would cut attendance by 40 students. Would this be a wise course to follow? Explain your answer on the back of this page.

Name _____   Date _____

Tyrel, Inc.

To earn money, Tyrel mows lawns, walks dogs, paints, and does errands for people in his neighborhood. Solve the following problems about Tyrel's work. If necessary, round your answers to the nearest cent.

1 Tyrel walks Mrs. Murray's dog each day for $10 per week. How much does he earn each day for walking the dog?

_____

2 Tyrel estimates that he can average $6.20 per hour throughout the week on all the jobs he does. Last week he worked $18\frac{3}{4}$ hours. If his estimate was correct, how much did he earn last week?

_____

If he worked a total of $84\frac{1}{2}$ hours last month and averaged $6.20 per hour, how much did he earn?

_____

3 With his earnings, Tyrel plans to buy an entertainment center for his room. The model he selected costs $804.44 (including tax). Last week, Tyrel earned an average of $7.28 per hour. At that rate, how many hours will he have to work to be able to buy the entertainment center?

_____

4 Tyrel mowed three lawns this past week. For the first, he earned $7.50, for the second he earned $9.25, and for the third he earned $12.50. If he spent a total of 4.5 hours working on these lawns, how much did he earn per hour?

5 Over the summer, Tyrel earned $965 mowing lawns. Unfortunately, this was not all profit. A tune-up for the mower at the beginning of the year cost $89.35, gasoline during the summer cost $75.98, and his mower broke down and cost $159.63 to repair. How much profit did Tyrel earn on his lawn-mowing service?

_____

6 Tyrel saves a fifth of his earnings each week. Last week his earnings were $124. How much did he save?

_____

7 Mr. Padillo asked Tyrel to paint the interior of his garage. Tyrel estimated that it would take him 5 hours to paint the garage. He told Mr. Padillo his fee would be $6.75 per hour, and that Mr. Padillo would have to buy the paint and materials. Four gallons of paint would be needed at a cost of $12.95 per gallon, and other materials would cost an additional $19.63. Mr. Padillo countered that he would prefer to pay Tyrel a flat fee of $100, but that Tyrel would then have to pay for the paint and materials. Which is the better deal for Tyrel? Explain your answer on the back of this page.

Name _____ Date _____

Lights Out!

Alvaro works part-time at a local department store. One day while he was working, his town experienced an electrical power outage because of a thunderstorm. Since the store had no backup power, the manager decided to close. Only the customers who were already in line to check out were able to do so. Alvaro, who was working as a checkout cashier, had to find the total cost of items and make change without the use of the cash register or even a calculator! Solve the following problems just like Alvaro had to.

1 Alvaro's first customer bought a package of 12 rolls of paper towels for $5.99 and a hairbrush for $6.99. What was the total cost of these purchases?

_____

The customer paid with a $20 bill. How much change should she receive?

_____

What is the least amount of bills and coins Alvaro should use to make the proper change?

_____

2 Alvaro's second customer bought a small hand shovel for $8.99, three bags of potting soil for $1.59 each, and two flowerpots for $4.69 each. What was the total cost of these purchases?

_____

The customer paid with a $50 bill. How much change should he receive?

_____

What is the least amount of bills and coins Alvaro should use to make the proper change?

_____

3 Alvaro's third customer bought a set of batteries for $3.99, a box of envelopes for $3.79, a package of loose-leaf paper for $3.69, and a solar calculator for $9.95. What was the total cost of these purchases?

_____

She paid with a $20 bill and a $10 bill. How much change should she receive?

_____

What is the least amount of bills and coins Alvaro should use to make the proper change?

_____

4 Alvaro's last customer bought $21.03 worth of items. At first the customer gave Alvaro $30, but then he game Alvaro $1.03 more for a total of $31.03. Why might he do this when the bill was $21.03? Explain your answer on the back of this page.

Around Town

After learning about ratios in school, Rashad realized how often ratios are used to describe mathematical relationships every day. Solve the following problems involving ratios. Express the ratios in simplest form.

1 Rashad helped his mother bake a cake for dessert. His mother told him that the recipe called for 3 cups of sugar for every 4 cups of flour. Write a ratio showing the relationship of sugar to flour.

_____

2 Rashad's basketball team finished their season having won 12 of 15 games. Write a ratio showing the number of games won to games lost.

_____

Write a ratio showing the number of games played to games lost.

_____

3 Rashad's brother plays ice hockey. In a recent game, his team took 20 shots and scored 3 goals. He scored 2 of the goals. Write a ratio showing the number of goals scored by Rashad 's brother to the total number of goals scored by his team.

_____

Write a ratio showing the shots taken by the team to the goals scored by his brother.

_____

4 Of the 180 students in Rashad's seventh-grade class, 96 are girls. Write a ratio showing the number of girls to boys in Rashad 's class.

_____

Write a ratio showing the number of students to boys in his class.

_____

5 Rashad read that half of the homes in his town have a pet. Write a ratio showing how many homes in his town have pets.

_____

He read that dogs account for a fourth of the pets in his town. Write a ratio showing the number of pet dogs in his town to the number of pets in his town.

_____

6 Rashad has 35 fish and 5 snails in his aquarium. He told his friend Heather that the ratio of fish to snails is 7 to 1. Heather says that the ratio is 35 to 5. On the back of this page, explain who (if either) is right.

Practice, Practice, Practice! Word Problems Scholastic Teaching Resources

Aunt Sarah's Bookstore

Finding Proportions

Aunt Sarah owns a bookstore. One day while helping in her aunt's store, Jenna found herself working with proportions almost as much as she worked selling books. Solve the following proportion problems based on Aunt Sarah's bookstore.

1 On a special sale day, Aunt Sarah offered her customers refreshments of cookies and punch. She asked Jenna to mix the punch. For every quart of punch, the recipe calls for 3 cups of ginger ale and 1 cup of fruit juice. Aunt Sarah asked Jenna to make 1 gallon (4 quarts) of punch. How many cups of ginger ale should Jenna use? How many cups of fruit juice?

_____

2 Yesterday, 4 out of every 10 people who came into the store bought at least 1 book. Aunt Sarah expects 200 customers today. If today's customers buy books in the same ratio as the customers of yesterday, at least how many books would Aunt Sarah expect to sell?

_____

If 300 people come to the store, at least how many books would she expect to sell?

_____

3 One out of every 10 books in Aunt Sarah's bookstore is fiction. A recent shipment contained 820 new books. Based on the ratio of 1 to 10, how many of the books were nonfiction?

_____

4 On a special two-day clearance sale, 3 out of 5 books on clearance were sold on the first day of the sale. If 280 books were originally for sale on clearance, how many were sold on the first day of the sale?

_____

Of the remaining books on the clearance sale, 3 out of 4 were sold the next day. How many books were not sold during those two days?

_____

5 On Saturday, Aunt Sarah ran a special sale on children's coloring books. If a customer bought two coloring books, he or she would get a third one free. When Jenna tallied the number of coloring books sold, plus the free books given out, the total was 321. What is the greatest possible number of customers who bought coloring books on the special sale?

_____

6 During the first hour her store was open, Aunt Sarah sold 18 books. If the store remained open 10 hours, Jenna assumed that Aunt Sarah would sell about 180 books. Is this a reasonable assumption to make? Explain your answer on the back of this page.

Practice, Practice, Practice! Word Problems • Scholastic Teaching Resources

23

Numbers by Many Names

Kerri and her friends at Morgan Middle School have found that fractions, decimals, and percents are closely related. Solve the following problems that show how the students use these numbers each day.

1 Some school lunches are more popular than others at Morgan Middle School. When hot dogs are served, $\frac{2}{5}$ of the students buy their lunch at school. When tacos are served, 36% of the students buy lunch. When pizza is served, 1.5 times as many students buy lunch than when tacos are served. If 650 students attend Morgan Middle School, how many order hot dogs for lunch?

_____

How many order tacos? _____

How many order pizza? _____

2 On their last math quiz, Taylor got 3 out of 4 problems correct. Roberto got 70% of the problems correct. Cara got three quarters of the problems right. Of the 25 problems on the quiz, Kerri had 5 mistakes. Whose score was the highest?

_____

Whose score was the lowest? _____

Which two students had the same score?

_____

3 Kerri plays the flute in the Morgan Advanced Band. Flute players make up 25% of the advanced band. The number of students who are taking beginner flute

lessons is 1.75 times the number of flute players in the advanced band. (Beginner flute students are not members of the advanced band yet.) If the advanced band has 96 students, how many currently play the flute in the advanced band?

_____

How many students are taking beginner flute lessons?

_____

4 Kerri's middle school has 650 students. The elementary school Kerri attended has 76% as many students as her middle school, and the high school in her town has 2.3 times as many students as her middle school. How many students attend Kerri's elementary school?

_____

How many attend the high school?

_____

5 Kerri's class had to find 25% of 24. Kerri changed 25% to 0.25 and multiplied by 24. Samantha, the math whiz, said that a shortcut to solve this problem was simply to divide 24 by 4. Can Samantha possibly be right? Explain your answer on the back of this page.

24

The Class Picnic

Luis volunteered to work with his class
Picnic Committee. Solve the following
percent problems related to the picnic.

1 Based on the attendance at past
picnics, Luis expects 95% of the students
in his class to attend this year's picnic. If
120 students are in the class, how many
students are likely to attend the picnic?

_____

2 When polled to find out if they
preferred hamburgers or hot dogs, all 120
students in the class responded. Sixty-five
percent said they preferred hamburgers,
while the rest preferred hot dogs. The
Picnic Committee decided to order 2
hamburgers or 2 hot dogs for each
student, based on the students' choices.
How many hamburgers were ordered?

_____

How many hot dogs
were ordered?   _____

3 When asked if they preferred cake or
ice cream for dessert, all 120 students
answered. Only 25% said they preferred
cake, while the rest preferred ice cream.
How many students preferred cake?

_____

Those who preferred ice cream were given
a choice of vanilla or chocolate. Sixty
percent preferred chocolate, 10% had no
preference, and the rest preferred vanilla.
How many preferred chocolate?

_____

How many preferred vanilla? _____

How many had no preference? _____

4 When asked if they preferred fruit
juice or spring water, all 120 students
answered. Fifty-five percent preferred
juice, and 45% preferred spring water.
The committee decided to order the
equivalent of 3 cups of juice for each
student who preferred juice. How many
gallons of juice should the committee
order? (16 cups equal 1 gallon.)

_____

The committee decided to order 2 bottles
of spring water for each student who
preferred water. How many bottles should
they order?

_____

5 After the picnic, Luis conducted a poll
to find out how many students enjoyed
the picnic. Of the 104 students who
responded, 25% rated it excellent, 60%
rated it good, 15% rated it fair, and 4%
rated it poor. Luis was pleased with these
results, but his teacher said that the
numbers could not be correct. Why not?
Explain your answer on the back of
this page.

Name _____ Date _____

Time for Hoops

Trish plays basketball in her town's basketball league. She learned that percents play a big part in understanding the game. Solve the following problems.

1 This year, Trish played in all of her team's games. The number of games Trish played in relation to the number of games the team played can be expressed as what percent?

_____

Last year, Trish injured her ankle and missed 25% of her team's games. If the team played 28 games, how many games did Trish miss because of her injury?

_____

2 Trish's team, the Hornets, played 24 games this season and won 62.5% of them. How many games did the Hornets win?

_____

The first-place team, the Vipers, won 75% of the 24 games they played. How many games did the Vipers win?

_____

3 Last season, Trish scored 70 points. This year she scored 160% more. How many points did Trish score this season?

_____

4 Trish attempted 32 free throws and made 75% of them. How many free throws did she make?

_____

The team attempted a total of 280 free throws and made 72.5% of them. How many free throws did the team make?

_____

5 375 people attended the championship game between the Hornets and the Vipers. 48% of those attending the game bought advance tickets. How many people bought advance tickets?

_____

6 During the season, Trish attempted 110 field goals and made 40% of them. How many field goals did Trish make?

_____

Her teammate Ellen attempted 120 field goals and made 37.5% of them. How many field goals did Ellen make?

_____

Sienna attempted 40 field goals and made 50% of them. How many field goals did Sienna make?

_____

In your opinion, which girl is the best scorer? Explain.

_____

_____

Name _____ Date _____

Play Ball!

Manuel enjoys playing baseball in his town's summer
baseball league. Like most baseball players, he understands how important math is to the game. Solve the
following percent problems related to baseball. If
necessary, round your answers to the nearest percent.

1 Manuel is a pitcher for his team, the
Warriors. In his last game he threw 80
pitches. Twenty-five were strikes. The
others were called balls. What percent of
the pitches were strikes?

_____

Of the 40 batters he faced, he walked 5.
What percent of the batters did he walk?

_____

2 To help meet its expenses, the league
sponsors a Donation Drive every June.
This year, Manuel and his teammates
collected $987 at the supermarket, $255
from a car wash (after the expenses were
paid), and $326 from a bake sale. What
percent of the total money collected did
the Warriors collect from the
supermarket?

_____

What percent of the total money collected
did they collect from the car wash?

_____

What percent of the total money collected
did they collect from the bake sale?

_____

3 At the end of every season, 36 players
are chosen to play in an all-star game. If
there are 10 teams with 18 players on
each team, what percent of the players are
chosen to play in the all-star game?

_____

Of the 36 players who were selected to
play in the all-star game this year, 30
actually played in the game. What percent
of the all-star players actually played in
the game?

_____

4 Will and Paul are twins who play on
the same team. They are excellent
ballplayers. Will got at least one hit in 12
out of 20 games in which he played. Paul
got at least one hit in 10 out of 20 games
he played. What percent of the games in
which Will played did he get at least one
hit?

_____

What percent of the games in which Paul
played did he get at least one hit?

_____

Can you say that at least one of the twins
got a hit in each of the 20 games they
played? Explain your answer on the back
of this page.

Name _____ Date _____

Reaching the Goal

Marissa is an eighth-grade student at North Mount Middle
School. Recently she took part in a fund-raising campaign for
her class. During the fund-raising effort, she learned how
mathematics can be used to find numbers if you know percents.

1 Every year the eighth-grade class raises
money for the class trip. So far, students
have raised $1,286, which is 40% of the
money they need. How much money is
their goal?

_____

How much more money
do they need to earn?   _____

2 To earn this extra money, students are
having a candy sale. Sixty-three students
made a total profit of $324, but only 35%
of the eighth-grade class participated in
the sale. How many students are in the
class?

_____

Find the average amount earned by each
student who participated in the sale.
(Round your answer to the nearest cent.)

_____

How much more money is needed for the
trip? (See Problem 1.)

_____

This is about what percent of their goal?

_____

3 The class has to raise this money
quickly, so they have decided to sponsor a
dance. A student DJ will provide the

music for $165. This amount is 75% of
the money the class had in the treasury
before any fund-raising efforts. How much
money was in the treasury?

_____

4 Each ticket for the dance costs $12.
One hundred and forty students were
expected to attend, but only 90% of these
did. How many students attended?

_____

This will not be enough. By how much
will the class fall short of their goal?

_____

To be sure they raised enough money,
how much should they have charged each
student who attended the dance? (See
Problem 2.)

_____

5 Many schools conduct fund-raisers to
earn money for special activities. Do you
think the methods of raising money that
were used in North Mount Middle School
were fair to all of the eighth-grade
students? Explain.

_____

_____

_____

28

Name _____ Date _____

A Special Promotion

Krystal just started working at a fast-food restaurant. Along with learning how to do her job, she also learned about percents of increase and decrease. Solve the problems. If necessary, round your answers to the nearest percent.

1 The manager of the restaurant where Krystal works is planning a big promotion. He plans to lower the price of hamburgers from $2.19 each to $1.79. What is the percent of decrease in the price of hamburgers?

_____

On the first day of the promotion, $635.45 worth of hamburgers were sold. How many hamburgers were sold?

_____

2 Usually about 320 medium sodas are sold between 11:00 A.M. and 2:00 P.M. on the weekend (Saturday and Sunday). During the promotion, 410 sodas were sold these two days. What was the percent of increase?

_____

During the promotion, about how many sodas were sold per hour between 11:00 A.M. and 2:00 P.M. on both days of the weekend? (Round your answer to the nearest whole number.)

_____

3 On the first day of the promotion, the number of chicken sandwiches decreased from 110 to 80. What is the percent of decrease?

_____

If a chicken sandwich sells for $2.49, what is the percent of decrease of the total sales of these sandwiches?

_____

4 Krystal was hired at a wage of $6.50 per hour. She worked 10 hours during the promotion. How much did she earn?

_____

Her boss gave her a $10 bonus. What percent of her earnings was the bonus?

_____

Krystal was later given a $0.50 increase in her hourly wage. What was the percent of increase in her hourly wage?

_____

5 An accountant analyzed sales at the restaurant during the promotion. He said that 2 out of every 3 people who came into the restaurant bought at least 1 hamburger. Krystal concluded that the number of hamburgers sold increased 50%. How do you think she decided this? Do you agree or disagree? Explain your answer on the back of this page.

29

Election Day

Kareem was the campaign manager for Alexis during her campaign for the seventh-grade class president at their school. As campaign manager, one of Kareem's biggest concerns was how students would vote. Solve the following problems that show the importance of percents. If necessary, round your answers to the nearest percent.

1 Kareem conducted a poll. Of 136 students in the seventh grade, 75% said they wanted the class president to be a spokesperson for the students. How many students wanted the class president to be a spokesperson?

_____

The poll indicated that 37.5% of the students believed that the class president should have a seat on the school board. How many students believed the president should have a seat on the school board?

_____

Twenty-five percent of the students believed that the class president should have a voice in determining the school's homework policy. How many students believed the president should have a voice in determining homework policy?

_____

2 Alexis was undecided if she should run for president. She was afraid of losing. Before placing her name on the ballot, her friends took an unofficial poll. Out of the 90 students polled, 50 said they would vote for her. What percent of the students polled said they would vote for Alexis?

_____

One week later, the same 90 students were polled, and 55 said they would vote for her. What is the percent of increase?

_____

3 Alexis was pleased with the results of these polls. She thought she could count on 55 out of 136 students if every student voted. What percent of the votes did she feel she could count on?

_____

Alexis figured that if every student who was not polled voted for her, she would win 101 out of 136 votes. This is about what percent of the total vote?

_____

4 Two days before the election, Kareem conducted a poll, asking students, "If the election were held today, which candidate would you vote for?" Only 92 students responded, with the following results: 52% for Jared, 46% for Alexis, and 2% undecided. Based on these results, Kareem concluded that Alexis's chances of winning the election were just as good as Jared's. Do you think he was being overly optimistic? Or was his conclusion reasonable? Explain your answer on the back of this page.

Name _____   Date _____

Shopping at the Mall

Tia loves to shop. That is why she was so interested to learn about discounts and sale prices. Buying items on sale saves money. Solve the following problems that Tia encountered the last time she went shopping at the mall. If necessary, round your answers to the nearest cent.

1 After visiting three stores in hopes of buying a pair of name-brand blue jeans, Tia found a pair she liked for $29.99. The jeans were discounted 15%. Find the amount of the discount and the sale price

discount: _____   sale price: _____

2 A pair of sneakers Tia liked originally cost $89.95, but they were discounted 25%. Find the amount of the discount and the sale price.

discount: _____   sale price: _____

3 Tia found a sweater that originally cost $39.79 but was discounted 30%. Find the amount of the discount and the sale price.

discount: _____   sale price: _____

4 At a music shop, Tia found the new CD of her favorite recording star. Originally priced at $19.95, the CD was discounted 20%. Find the amount of the discount and the sale price.

discount: _____   sale price: _____

5 A backpack Tia liked cost $34.99 but was discounted 5%. Find the amount of the discount and the sale price.

discount: _____   sale price: _____

6 After searching for a new handbag, Tia found one she liked that cost $21.95. It was discounted 10%. Find the amount of the discount and the sale price.

discount: _____   sale price: _____

7 Tia looked in several stores for a pair of gloves. She finally found a pair she liked. The list price of the gloves was $24.99, but the gloves were discounted 10%. If Tia paid cash, she would receive an additional 5% off the discounted price. In another store, she found the same gloves for a price of $24.99, discounted 15%. Which store offered the better price, or were they the same? Explain.

_____

_____

_____

_____

Practice, Practice, Practice! Word Problems   Scholastic Teaching Resources

31

Moving to the Burbs

Nicki's family recently purchased a new home in the suburbs. After moving in, Nicki and her father went to buy materials and equipment to care for the lawn. Nicki learned a lot about lawn care and sales tax. Solve the following problems. If necessary, round your answers to the nearest cent.

1 To fill in some bare spots in the lawn, Nicki and her father bought grass seed for $65.95. The sales tax was 5%. What was the total cost of the grass seed?

_____

2 Next, Nicki and her father bought fertilizer for $79.49. The sales tax was 5%. What was the total cost of the fertilizer?

_____

3 To water the new grass seed, Nicki and her father bought a hose for $18.99 and a sprinkler for $6.99. The sales tax for these items was 4.5%. What was the total cost of the hose?

_____

What was the total cost of the sprinkler?

_____

4 They decided they would also need garden tools. The cost of this equipment was $57.95. The sales tax was 4.5%. What was the total cost of the equipment?

_____

5 Thinking ahead to fall when they would have to clear leaves, Nicki and her father bought a leaf blower for $89.59. The sales tax was 5%. What was the total cost of the leaf blower?

_____

Last year, the sales tax on leaf blowers was 4.3%. If they had purchased the same model leaf blower last year for the same price ($89.59), how much money would they have saved in sales tax?

_____

6 Because their lawn is so big, Nicki's father wants to buy a riding mower. The model he likes costs $2,895.95. The sales tax on this mower in their state is 5%. In a neighboring state, the sales tax on the mower is 3.5%. Nicki's father is considering buying the mower there, but the round-trip is 150 miles. His pickup truck gets 21 miles per gallon of gas, and gas costs $1.80 per gallon. Do you think the savings in sales tax is enough to justify making the trip to buy the mower in the next state? Explain your answer on the back of this page.

Practice, Practice, Practice! Word Problems   Scholastic Teaching Resources

Name _____   Date _____

Cashing in Big

Cal works at a part-time job after school. He wants to buy a car in a few years, and he saves as much money as he can. He puts money in a savings account at a local bank where his money earns simple interest. Use the following formula to solve the problems: $I = p \times r \times t$

I = interest

p = principal, the amount of money in the account

r = rate, the percent of interest paid

t = time, the length of time money is in the account

Note that the rate and time must be in the same unit. For the problems below, express time in years. If necessary, round your answers to the nearest cent.

1 Cal opened his savings account with $300. The yearly rate of interest was $2\frac{1}{2}$%. The interest was computed every 3 months. Cal set up the problem like this:

$I = p \times r \times t$

$I = \$300 \times 0.025 \times 0.25$

How much interest did Cal earn after 3 months?

_____

2 After a year, Cal had $480 in his account. The interest rate rose to $2\frac{3}{4}$%. The interest was computed every 3 months. How much interest did he earn after 3 months?

_____

Assuming the interest rate did not change, how much interest did he earn after one year?

_____

3 Learning that the interest rate at another bank was $3\frac{1}{4}$%, Cal closed his first account and opened a savings account at the new bank. He deposited $600. Both banks computed interest every 3 months. Since the first bank's interest rate was $2\frac{3}{4}$%, how much more interest did Cal earn after 3 months at the new bank?

_____

4 Cal and his sister Kelli both had savings accounts. Cal deposited $360 at an interest rate of $2\frac{3}{4}$%, computed every 3 months. Kelli deposited $400 at an interest rate of $2\frac{1}{2}$%, computed every 3 months. At the end of three months, Cal had earned $2.48 in interest and Kelli had earned $2.50. Pleased that she had earned more, Kelli told Cal that her rate of interest was better than his. Cal disagreed. Who is right? Explain your answer on the back of this page.

33

Time to Remodel

Cheryl's parents are remodeling their home. They told Cheryl that after her room is finished, she can have all new furniture. When her parents helped her to pick her furniture, Cheryl learned about loans and interest. Solve the problems that follow. Use the formula $I = p \times r \times t$. If necessary, round answers to the nearest cent.

1 The new rug in Cheryl's room costs $295. Her parents borrowed the full amount of the cost of the rug at an interest rate of 8% for 4 years. How much interest did they pay?

_____

What was the total amount they paid for the rug after 4 years?

_____

2 Cheryl's new bedroom set costs $995.79. Her parents paid $200 and agreed to finance the rest of the amount at an interest rate of 7.5% for 4 years. How much interest did they pay?

_____

What was the total amount they paid for the bedroom set after 4 years?

_____

3 Cheryl's new stereo system costs $449.69. Her parents paid $100 of the total and decided to finance the rest of the amount at an interest rate of 9% for 3 years. How much interest did they pay?

_____

How much interest did they save by making a down payment of $100?

_____

4 If Cheryl's parents did not borrow any money to pay for the rug, furniture, and stereo system, how much would they have saved in interest? (See Problems 1, 2, and 3.)

_____

5 Cheryl's older brother, Jeff, is thinking of buying a car. He has $2,500 for a down payment and must borrow $5,000. He can borrow the money at Smith Bank at an interest rate of 8% per year for 4 years. At Jones Bank he can borrow the money at $7\frac{1}{2}$% for 5 years. The monthly payment at Jones Bank is a little less than the monthly payment at Smith Bank. Jeff told Cheryl that he thinks the loan at Jones Bank is the better deal because the interest rate is lower. She says that the loan from Smith Bank is better deal. Who is right? Explain.

_____

_____

_____

A Fish Story

When his parents told him they were buying an aquarium for the family room, Jason was willing to help set it up. He soon found out that more goes into a fish tank than just fish. Solve the following problems. If necessary, round your answers to the nearest cent.

1 One tank Jason's parents considered buying held 50 gallons of water and cost $209.69. It was discounted 25%. What was the amount of the discount?

_____

What was the sale
price of this tank? _____

His parents would also have to pay a sales tax of 3.5%. What was the total cost of the tank?

_____

2 To complete the aquarium, they needed to buy several items:

    air pump, $54.99
    power filter, $46.99
    heater, $26.95
    light, $14.79
    5 bags of gravel at $1.89 each

Sales tax on these items was 3.5%. What was the total cost of the these items?

_____

3 After considering buying the tank and equipment separately, Jason's father considered buying a complete aquarium system. This included a 60-gallon tank and all of the other necessary equipment. It even included fish that would be

shipped after the aquarium was set up. The cost of this complete aquarium was $495.79. If Jason's parents decided to buy this system, they could pay $100 now and borrow the rest of the cost at an interest rate of 8% for 3 years. How much interest would they pay for the amount they borrowed?

_____

How much would they
pay in all for this system? _____

4 After successfully setting up an aquarium in the family room, Jason would like to set one up in his room. He can buy a 30-gallon tank with all the necessary equipment at a local store. The list price is $89.95, but the store offers a discount of 15%. He would have to pay 3.5% sales tax. On an Internet site, he can buy the same aquarium and equipment at $\frac{1}{4}$ off the list price. There is no sales tax, but he would have to pay $10 for shipping. If you were Jason, which would you choose? Explain.

_____

_____

_____

_____

Name _____   Date _____

Kim's Averages

Finding Averages

Kim liked to keep track of her test scores so that she could find her test average in each of her subjects. As the end of the marking period neared, she averaged her test grades. Find the averages of the test scores below and answer the questions. If necessary, round averages to the nearest tenth.

1 In math, Kim's test scores for the marking period were 88, 92, 95, 100, and 96. What was her test average in math?

_____

2 In science, her test scores for the marking period were 80, 84, 86, 75, and 82. What was her test average in science?

_____

3 In history, Kim's test scores for the marking period were 86, 94, 98, and 88. What was her test average in history?

_____

The test average, class participation, and homework each make up $\frac{1}{3}$ of her grade in history. Kim's class participation grade is 90 and her homework grade is 88. What was Kim's overall average for the class this marking period?

_____

4 In language arts, Kim's test scores for the marking period were 82, 86, and 93. What was her test average in language arts?

_____

Test scores, a term paper, homework, and class participation each count for a quarter of her grade in language arts. Kim received 92 on her term paper, 85 for class participation, and 90 for homework. What was Kim's overall average for the class this marking period?

_____

5 Kim's friend Carl is very concerned about his math grade. Since his teacher counts tests heavily toward a student's grade, Carl figures that if he has an A test average (an average of 90 or above), he will receive an A on his report card. The scores on his first four math tests of the marking period were 92, 94, 92, and 90. Carl averaged these grades and found the average to be 92. The score on his next test was 82. When he added this to his current average of 92, his average fell to 87. (92 + 82 = 174; 174 ÷ 2 = 87) When Carl told Kim how he found his average, Kim smiled and said, "Don't worry. You'll get an A." Was Kim right? Explain.

_____

_____

_____

36

Practice, Practice, Practice! Word Problems   Scholastic Teaching Resources

Name _____   Date _____

Running Out of Time

Between school, sports, and working a few hours each week in Mr. Wallace's sandwich shop, Matt never seems to have enough time. Solve the following problems related to time.

1 Last night Matt went to sleep at 10:30 P.M. and woke up at 7:15 A.M. How long did he sleep?

_____

Many doctors recommend at least 8 hours of sleep each night for a student of Matt's age. How much more, or less, sleep than 8 hours did Matt get last night?

_____

What fractional part
of an hour is this? _____

2 After school yesterday, Matt attended soccer practice from 3:15 P.M. to 5:00 P.M. Then he returned home and worked on homework from 5:30 to 6:45. After that he ate dinner. After dinner, he worked on homework for another 35 minutes. How much time did Matt spend at soccer practice and doing homework yesterday?

_____

3 On a recent trip, Matt's class visited a museum. They arrived at the museum at 10:45 A.M. The class stayed for 4 hours. The bus trip back to school took 1 hour and 20 minutes. What time did Matt and his classmates return to school?

_____

4 Last week Matt worked in Mr. Wallace's sandwich shop three days. He worked 2 hours and 15 minutes after school on Monday, 2 hours and 45 minutes on Wednesday, and 3 hours and 15 minutes on Saturday. How long did he work last week?

_____

If Matt was paid $6.50 per hour, how much did he earn last week? (Round your answer to the nearest cent.)

_____

5 This coming Saturday, Matt has a very busy day. He plans to wake up at 9:30 A.M. He is scheduled to work in the sandwich shop from 10:30 A.M. to 1:30 P.M. He has soccer practice from 2:30 to 4:30. His mom wants him to watch his little brother from 5:00 to 6:00, after which the family will eat dinner. At 7:00, Matt plans to go to a birthday party at his friend's house. Matt also needs to do about 2 hours of research on the Internet for his science report. Is this a practical schedule? If not, what might Matt do to make it more practical? Explain your answer on the back of this page.

Name _____   Date _____

Down on the Farm

Kirsten enjoys helping her father and mother on their farm. One of the many things she has learned is the importance of measurement. Solve the following problems. If necessary, refer to your math book for the values of the units of customary measures.

1 Shadow, Kirsten's new puppy, gained 4 pounds 7 ounces last month. The veterinarian says that Shadow will probably gain about this much weight for each of the next four months. If Shadow weighs $15\frac{1}{2}$ pounds now, about how much will he weigh in four months?

2 Kirsten's mother asked her to pick 3 pounds of apples for apple pie. If each apple weighed 4 ounces, how many apples should Kirsten pick?

3 Kirsten helped her father build an addition to the deck at the back of their house. The addition was 7 feet 11 inches on one side and $8\frac{1}{2}$ feet on the other. They want to put a safety rail on these two sides. What is the total length of rail they should buy?

4 To keep livestock on their property, Kirsten's father will fence in a section of land. He figures he will need about $\frac{1}{4}$ mile of fencing. If he buys the fence in sections of 8 feet, how many sections of fence will he need to buy?

5 On a very hot day last week, Kirsten's father and three helpers were working to repair the barn roof. Kirsten made a gallon of lemonade and served the men in plastic cups that each held 1 pint. How many 1-pint servings are in a gallon?

Frank drank $2\frac{1}{2}$ pints, Dave drank $1\frac{1}{2}$ pints, Pete drank 2 pints, and Kirsten's father drank $1\frac{1}{2}$ pints. How much lemonade was left?

6 Kirsten's father measured a section of lawn that needed to be reseeded. The section was 6 yards wide by 12 yards long. He asked Kirsten to calculate this area in square feet. Kirsten multiplied 6 yards times 12 yards and got 72 square yards. She then multiplied this by 3 because 3 feet equal 1 yard. She told her father they needed to buy enough grass seed to cover 216 square feet. Explain what is wrong with this answer.

Name _____ Date _____

Think Metric

Many products in the U.S. are labeled with both metric and customary units of measurement. By thinking metric, it is easier to learn the metric system. Solve the following problems. If necessary, refer to your math book for the values of metric units.

1 Mike was helping his father put edging around the flower bed in the front of their home. The edging was packed in sections of 350 centimeters. How many meters is this?

_____

If they needed 9.35 meters of edging, how many sections would they have to buy?

_____

How much edging would be left over? _____

2 For lunch, Mike enjoys peanut butter sandwiches. In two weeks he used 680 grams of peanut butter out of a 1-kilogram jar. How much was left in the jar?

_____

What part of a kilogram was left in the jar? _____

3 On a recent trip, Mike noticed that the speedometer in his mother's car was labeled both in miles per hour and kilometers per hour. They drove to his grandmother's house. The total distance was 294 kilometers. The drive took 3

hours and 30 minutes. What was their average speed in kilometers per hour?

_____

4 Some of Alicia's friends were coming to visit her. Mike went with her to the store to buy refreshments. A 640-gram bag of pretzels was on sale for $2.59. A 1-kilogram box of pretzels was priced at $5.49. Which was the better buy?

_____

Alicia also wanted to buy spring water for her friends. She considered buying a six-pack of 355-milliliter bottles or one 2-liter bottle of spring water. Which contained more water, the six-pack or the 2-liter bottle? How much more?

_____

5 Many people consider the metric system to be easier to use than other measurement systems. Why? Explain.

_____

_____

_____

_____

Name _____ Date _____

Moving In

Latrice and her family recently moved into a new home. As they did, Latrice learned how important understanding measurement can be. Solve the problems below. If necessary, refer to your math book for the values of the units of measures.

1 Latrice's new home is 15 kilometers from her old home. She and her family averaged 60 kilometers per hour driving from their old home to their new one. How long did the drive take?

_____

2 The family started moving in at 9:35 A.M. and finished at 3:15 P.M. They stopped from 12:15 to 1:00 for lunch. How long did they work to move in?

_____

3 Latrice and her sister each had her own room. Latrice, being older, got the bigger room. Although both rooms were 3.4 meters wide, Latrice's room was 4.2 meters long. Her sister's room was 3.85 meters long. How many meters longer was Latrice's room?

_____

How many centimeters is this?

_____

4 Latrice's mother planned to make curtains for eight of the windows in their new home. She will need $1\frac{1}{3}$ yards of material for each window. (The fabric she will buy is wide enough for each window.)

How much fabric will she need to buy?

_____

How many feet is this? _____

5 Latrice and her family decided to invite friends and relatives to visit their new home. Latrice's mother asked Latrice to make enough punch for 30 1-cup servings. Latrice made 2 gallons of punch. Assuming the guests would drink 30 cups of punch, did Latrice make enough?

_____

If yes, how much extra did she make?

_____

If not, how many cups short would she be? _____

6 Latrice placed a flower stand in front of the window in her room. The flower stand holds five plants with a total weight of 7.5 kilograms. The plants Latrice wishes to place on the stand weigh the following: 1.5 kilograms, 2.25 kilograms, 1.3 kilograms, 2.36 kilograms, and 670 grams. Will the flower stand be able to support the combined weight of these five plants? Explain your answer on the back of this page.

Name _____   Date _____

Lori the Landscaper

Lori helps her father with his landscaping business whenever she can. She understands measurement, which is an important skill for the work she does. Answer the following questions. Use the following formulas: $P = s + s + s + s$ and $A = l \times w$.

1 When Lori's father got a job to enclose a yard with a fence, he asked her to help him find how much fencing they would need. The area to be fenced was a rectangle, 102 feet by 96 feet. Her father told Lori that the gate for the driveway would be 12 feet wide and should not be included with the total amount of fencing needed. How many feet of fencing would they need to enclose the yard?

_____

The fence the customer wanted came in sections of 8 feet. How many sections have to be ordered?

_____

Each section costs $15.99. How much will the fence cost?

_____

2 The next job involved reseeding a customer's lawn. Only the backyard and front yard needed reseeding. The dimensions of the backyard were 98 feet by 64 feet. What was the area of the backyard?

_____

A patio with dimensions of 16 feet by 14 feet was also in the backyard. What was the area of the patio?

Since grass seed was not needed for the area covered by the patio, what was the area of the backyard that had to be reseeded?

_____

The dimensions of the front lawn were 42 feet by 48 feet. What was the area of the front lawn?

_____

What was the total area of the yard that had to be reseeded?

_____

3 One of their customers asked Lori and her dad to make a rectangular flowerbed 16 feet long by 12 feet wide. What was the area of the flowerbed?

_____

To provide good coverage, 3 flowers should be planted for every square foot. How many flowers should be planted in the flowerbed?

_____

The customer would also like plastic edging to be placed around the flowerbed. Assuming the edging is placed on each side, how much edging is needed?

_____

Name _____   Date _____

Carissa's Circles

After having learned about circles in school, Carissa noticed that circles are found just about everywhere. Solve the following problems. Use the formulas: $C = \pi \times d$ and $A = \pi \times r^2$. Use 3.14 for π. Round your answers to the nearest hundredth if necessary.

1 Carissa's parents want to plant a circular flower garden that has a diameter of 10 feet. What will be the area of the flower garden?

_____

If they place edging along the flower garden, how many feet of edging will they need?

_____

2 Carissa's parents also want to buy a pool for their backyard. The circular pool they are considering has a diameter of 16 feet. Her father wants to spread sand under the pool to use as a base. What is the area the sand will cover?

_____

Her mother wants a circular deck around the pool. The deck will extend 4 feet outward from the edge of the pool, making the diameter of the deck 24 feet. They want to buy decorative lights to place around the outside edge of the deck. How many feet of wiring will they need?

_____

3 Carissa's father is remodeling the attic and would like to install a circular window for ventilation. The window has a

diameter of 1.5 feet. What is the area of the window in square inches?

_____

He plans to place a strip of insulation around the edge of the window. How many inches long should the strip of insulation be if he is to seal the entire window?

_____

He decides to install a larger window with a diameter of 2 feet. Find the difference in the areas of the windows.

_____

Assuming he uses the same kind of insulation around this window, how much insulation will he need?

_____

4 Carissa wants to buy her dog, Ozzie, a new bed. His old rectangular bed was 36 inches by 32 inches. Ozzie fits on his old bed just about perfectly. A new circular bed with a diameter of 34 inches is on sale. Carissa likes the circular bed, but she is afraid it might be too small for Ozzie. If you were Carissa, which bed would you choose? Explain your answer on the back of this page.

Name _____ Date _____

Moving Out

Genaro and his parents are moving. Moving to a new home is exciting, but it is also a lot of work, as Genaro found out when he began helping his parents pack. Solve the following problems. Use the formula $V = l \times w \times h$.

1 Genaro's parents plan to place some items in a storage unit. The storage unit is 10 feet long, 12 feet high, and 5 feet wide. What is the volume of this storage unit?

_____

A larger storage unit is 20 feet long, 12 feet high, and 10 feet wide. How much more volume does this storage unit have than the smaller one?

_____

2 Genaro's mother wants to pack various small items in 1-cubic-foot boxes. She plans to pack these small boxes in bigger boxes that measure 3 feet long, 2 feet high, and 2 feet wide. How many 1-cubic-foot boxes can she pack in each larger box?

_____

If she decides to pack the 1-cubic-foot boxes in a box that is 4 feet long, 2 feet high, and 2 feet wide, how many 1-cubic-foot boxes can she pack?

_____

3 Genaro wants to pack his encyclopedias in storage crates. Each crate is 1.5 feet long, 10 inches high, and 14 inches wide. How many cubic inches does each crate contain?

_____

His encyclopedia set contains 24 books. He can fit 18 books in one storage crate and 6 others in a second crate. Assuming the first crate is filled, how much space is left in the second crate?

_____

4 Genaro owns a collection of model cars. Each car is stored in a box that is 3 inches long, 2 inches high, and 2.5 inches wide. He has 40 cars and wishes to pack them in a large box. Estimate the volume of a box that would be big enough to hold the 40 model cars.

_____

5 Genaro's father had a box 2 feet long, 1 foot high, and 1 foot wide in which to pack items from the garage. After packing some of the items, Genaro and his father found that the box was not big enough. Genaro suggested that they use another box that was twice as long, twice as high, and twice as wide. He said that this box would have twice the volume as the first box. Was he right? Explain your answer on the back of this page.

43

Packing Up

Teena's mother owns a gift shop. Sometimes Teena helps in the shop by wrapping packages. Solve the following problems.

1 One of the biggest boxes Teena had to wrap was 3 feet long, 2.5 feet wide, and 1.5 feet high. How much wrapping paper was needed to cover the box?

_____

2 Teena had to wrap another box, which was 20 inches long, 3 inches high, and 2 inches wide. What was the surface area of this box?

_____

She had a section of wrapping paper that was 48 inches long and 12 inches wide. Did she have enough paper to wrap the box? If yes, how much paper, if any, did she have left over?

_____

If no, how much paper was she short?

_____

3 A customer wanted a package wrapped with two kinds of paper. The box was 14 inches long, 6 inches high, and 8 inches wide. The top of the box was 14 inches by 8 inches. The customer wanted solid blue wrapping paper for the top, and red wrapping paper for the rest of the box. What was the least amount of blue wrapping paper needed?

_____

What was the least amount of red wrapping paper needed?

_____

4 One Saturday, Teena and her mother decided to paint the stockroom in the back of the shop. They wanted to paint four walls and the ceiling white. The room was 15 feet long, 12 feet high, and 10 feet wide. The door was also to be painted white. Find the total area that needs to be painted.

_____

A gallon of white paint covers 410 square feet. Assuming that the room required only one coat of paint, how much paint should they buy to paint the room?

_____

5 Teena had two boxes to wrap. One was 3 inches by 5 inches by 2 inches, and the other was 6 inches by 5 inches by 1 inch. Teena assumed that since these boxes had the same volume, they would have the same surface area. Do they? Explain your answer on the back of this page.

James and Geometry

When James's family began remodeling their home, James found the geometry he had learned in school to be very helpful. Solve the following problems. Use 3.14 for π. If necessary, round your answers to the nearest hundredth.

1 After remodeling the three upstairs bedrooms, James's parents decided to buy new rugs for each room. Each room was rectangular. The first room was 18 feet by 14 feet. The second room was 12 feet 6 inches by 10 feet. The third room was 9 feet 9 inches by 9 feet. What was the area of the first room?

_____

What was the total area of the three rooms?

_____

2 James and his father built a fishpond in the backyard. The rectangular pond was 4 feet long, 3 feet deep, and 3.5 feet wide. If water is to fill the pond to a depth of 2.5 feet, how much water (in cubic inches) will be needed?

_____

About how many gallons of water is this? (The volume of 1 gallon of water equals about 231 cubic inches.)

_____

3 James's mother would like to make a circular flower garden near the fishpond. The garden is to be 5 feet in diameter. What is the area of the garden?

James's father suggests placing plastic edging around the garden. How much edging should they buy to go around the garden?

_____

4 The family would also like to fence in a rectangular area for Butch, their dog, to run. The area to be fenced in is 64 feet by 28 feet. Not including the gate, which is 4 feet wide, how many feet of fence will they need to buy?

_____

5 James's father asked James to repaint a wooden crate that was used for storage. The crate was 4 feet long, 30 inches high, and 2 feet wide. What was the surface area of the crate?

_____

6 James's mother would like to tile the foyer by the front door. The foyer is a square with sides 8 feet long. The tiles are squares with sides 8 inches long. James estimates that they will need 144 tiles. On the back of this page, explain how he got this answer and decide if he is correct.

Practice, Practice, Practice! Word Problems   Scholastic Teaching Resources

45

Name _____ Date _____

Surf's Up!

Kristen's parents own a surf shop. One day while Kristen was helping in the shop, her mother and father were tallying the number of surfboards they sold during the year. Kristen suggested that they use a line graph to represent the data. Study the line graph, then solve the problems.

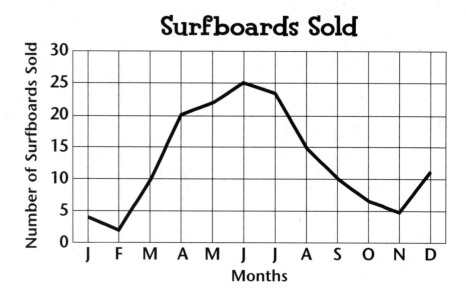

Surfboards Sold

1 In which month were the greatest number of surfboards sold?

_____

How many were sold this month?

_____

2 In which month were the least number of surfboards sold?

_____

How many were sold this month?

_____

3 In which three successive months did the sale of surfboards increase the most?

_____

4 In which three successive months did the sale of surfboards decrease the most?

_____

5 How many surfboards were sold in May? _____

How many surfboards were sold in August? _____

How many surfboards were sold in October? _____

6 According to the graph, what are the two best months for selling surfboards?

_____

7 During which season are the fewest surfboards sold?

_____

8 Describe the pattern of surfboard sales. What might be the reasons for this pattern?

_____

_____

_____

Name ______________________ Date ______________

Time for Lunch

Interpreting Bar Graphs

Ashlee is a member of her school's eighth-grade student council. As chairperson of the council's Lunch Committee, Ashlee conducted a poll among seventh- and eighth-grade students to find out which lunches students preferred. She graphed her results. Study the graph and answer the questions that follow. Round your answers to the nearest percent.

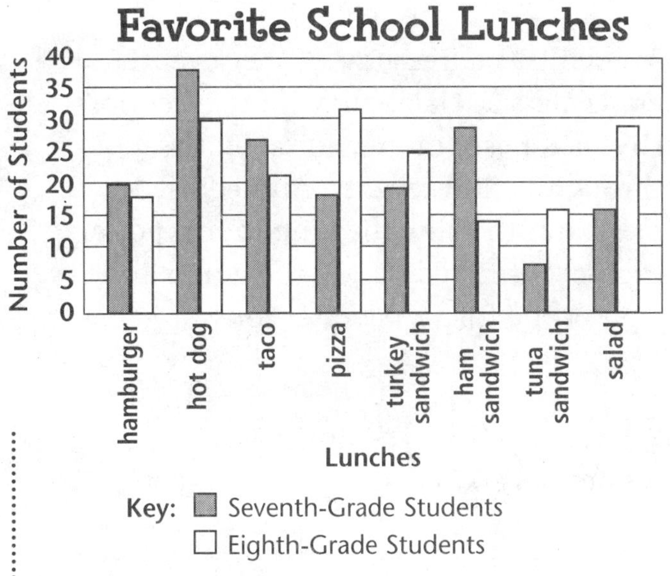

Total Number of Students

Seventh Grade: 172 Eighth Grade: 180

1 What is the most popular lunch among seventh graders? How many seventh graders prefer this lunch?

____

What is the most popular lunch among eighth graders? How many eighth graders prefer this lunch?

____

2 What is the least popular lunch among seventh graders? How many seventh graders prefer this lunch?

____

What is the least popular lunch among eighth graders? How many eighth graders prefer this lunch?

____

3 How many more seventh graders than eighth graders prefer ham sandwiches?

____

How many more eighth graders than seventh graders prefer pizza?

____

4 What percentage of seventh-grade students prefer hamburgers or hot dogs for lunch?

____

What percentage of eighth graders prefer pizza or hot dogs for lunch?

____

What percentage of the students in both grades prefer hot dogs for lunch?

____

5 Each year the cafeteria staff changes the menu based on the preferences of the students. The student council Lunch Committee was asked which two lunches should be replaced for next year. Based on the data, if you were Ashlee, which two lunches would you recommend be replaced next year? Explain your answer on the back of this page.

Name _____ Date _____

A Piece of the Pie

Ahmed is the treasurer of the seventh-grade class at Oak Valley Middle School. His class raises money for activities through various events. Ahmed used a pie graph to show the amount of money each event raised. Study the graph and answer the following questions.

7th Grade Fund-Raising Events

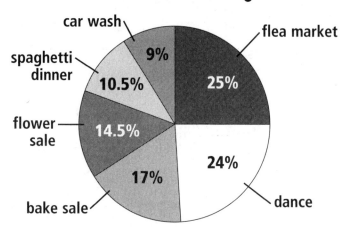

Total Amount Raised: $2,440

1 What percentage of the total money was raised at the flea market?

_____

How much money was raised at the flea market?

_____

2 What percentage of the total money was raised at the car wash?

_____

How much money was raised at the car wash?

_____

3 How much more money was raised at the flea market than at the car wash?

_____

4 How much money was raised at the bake sale?

_____

How much more money was raised at the dance than at the bake sale?

_____

5 Find the difference between the money raised at the flower sale and at the spaghetti dinner.

_____

6 Ahmed offered a suggestion for next year. Since the flea market and dance raised about half of the total amount of money, he feels that the class should have two dances and two flea markets instead of the car wash and spaghetti dinner. Do you agree? Explain.

_____

_____

_____

_____

_____

_____

_____

Name _____ Date _____

Picture This

Vanessa's school has a problem: overcrowded classes. Vanessa and her mother have organized a committee of parents and students to urge the members of their board of education to reduce the number of students in the classes in Vanessa's school. They gathered information on the average class sizes in the six other schools in town and plan to show their data at the next board of education meeting. To present their data clearly, Vanessa helped her mother design a pictograph. Study the graph and answer the questions.

Average Class Sizes in Local Schools

Hill School	☺☺☺☺☺☺☺☺☺☺
McDermott School	☺☺☺☺☺☺
River School	☺☺☺☺☺☺☺☺
Petersen School	☺☺☺☺☺☺☺☺☺
Plainview School	☺☺☺☺☺☺
Rosemont School	☺☺☺☺☺☺☺☺☺☺☺
Wallace School	☺☺☺☺☺

Key: ☺ = 3 students

1 How many students does each symbol on the graph represent?

_____

2 Which school has the smallest average class size?

_____

3 Which school has the largest average class size?

_____

4 Vanessa goes to Hill School. On average, how many students does Hill School have in each class?

_____

5 On average, how many students does McDermott School have in each class?

_____

6 Which two schools' combined average class size is about the same as Rosemont's?

_____

7 After showing this graph to the members of the school board, one of the members of the board pointed out that the pictograph showed average class sizes. He argued that averages could be misleading. For example, a few classes with a low number of students can reduce the average class size of a whole school. A few classes with a large number of students can increase the average class size for an entire school. Do you think his point is valid? Explain.

_____

_____

_____

Name _____ Date _____

The Chances Are. . .

Recently Michael's school held its annual fund-raising spring fair. There were amusements, contests, and plenty of games to play. Michael especially liked the games of chance where he hoped to beat the odds. Solve the problems that follow.

1 One of the most popular attractions at the fair was the magician. Michael and 35 other students attended the first show. The magician needed one student assistant. All of the students present volunteered. What was the probability of Michael being selected?

_____

If the magician needed two student volunteers to help him, and all of the students present volunteered, what was the probability of Michael being chosen?

_____

If the magician needed three volunteers, what was the probability of Michael being chosen?

_____

2 Twenty-five students, including Michael, participated in the potato sack race. Assuming all of the racers had roughly the same ability, what was the probability of Michael being the winner of the race?

_____

Five separate races were scheduled, with five students taking part in each race. Michael was in the first race. What was the probability he would win this race?

_____

The winners of the first five races would then race. The student who came in first in this last race would receive a blue ribbon. Michael was in this race. What was the probability now that he would win the blue ribbon?

_____

3 Michael played a wheel of chance where the winners could pick books for prizes. Twelve numbers were on the wheel. If Michael placed a token on one number, what was the probability he would win?

_____

If he played two tokens (on different numbers), what was the probability he would win?

_____

4 Michael enjoys games of chance where some skill is involved. He observed a ringtoss game in which players tossed small rings, hoping to encircle them around the neck of a bottle. Michael found that 12 different players made 63 tosses before somebody won. Michael concluded that his odds of winning were $\frac{1}{63}$. Is this a valid conclusion? Explain your answer on the back of this page.

Practice, Practice, Practice! Word Problems   Scholastic Teaching Resources

Scoring with Integers

Steve is the quarterback for the Falcons, his school's football team. Football is a sport in which integers are important not just for keeping score but also for keeping track of yards lost and gained. Solve the following problems.

1 In the Falcons' first game of the season, they got the ball on their own 20-yard line. On their first play from scrimmage, they lost 3 yards. On the second play, they gained 2 yards. On the third play, they lost 5 yards. Write an integer to represent the total yardage gained or lost on these three plays.

_____

On what yard line was the ball after these three plays?

_____

2 Last year, Steve completed the longest pass of his career, gaining 32 yards. In the second quarter of his first game this year, Steve completed a pass that was only 3 yards short of his personal best last year. How many yards did this completed pass gain?

_____

3 Bryan, one of Steve's friends, is a running back for the Falcons. During the game, Bryan ran the ball eight times and gained or lost the following yards: gained 2 yards, gained 6, lost 5, gained 17, gained 4, lost 2, gained 9, and gained 1.

How many yards did he gain in the game?

_____

What was his average gain per run?

_____

4 Eddie, another one of Steve's friends, is also a running back. Eddie ran the ball three times but lost a total of 7 yards. He also caught five passes, for an average gain of 4 yards per pass. Between pass catching and running, how many total yards did Eddie gain?

_____

5 In the last quarter of the game, the score was tied. The Falcons were on the 50-yard line. (Remember that the distance from goal line to goal line on a football field is 100 yards.) In the final eight plays of the game, the Falcons gained or lost the following yards: gained 13 yards, lost 5, lost 3, gained 26, gained 3, lost 4, gained 14, and gained 6. Would they have scored a touchdown? Explain.

_____

_____

_____

Name _____   Date _____

Class Trip to Disney World!

Lucas is an eighth grader at Big River Middle School. Each May, the eighth-grade class goes on a three-day trip to Disney World. Solve the following problems.

1 The number of students going on the eighth-grade class trip has been decreasing at an average rate of 6 students per year for the last five years. Write an integer that represents the total decrease over this time period.

_____

If at least 20 more students decide not to go, school officials are thinking of canceling the trip. If the current rate of decrease continues, in how many years may the trip be canceled?

_____

2 Part of the reason for the decline in the numbers of students going on the trip is the increasing cost. The cost of the trip has been rising at an average rate of $7 per year for the last five years. Write an integer that represents the total increase in costs over this time period.

_____

If the cost of the trip five years ago was $180, what is the current cost of the trip?

_____

3 One of the ways the eighth grade helps to pay for the trip is to sell boxes of greeting cards and holiday wrapping paper. The cards cost $3 per box and the wrapping paper costs $6 per roll. Lucas

sold several boxes of cards and several rolls of wrapping paper. When it came time to turn in the money for his orders, two people owed him money for 1 box of cards each, and three people owed him money for 1 roll of wrapping paper each. In relation to the money Lucas collected, write an integer that represents the total money he was still owed.

_____

4 Lucas borrowed $80 from his mother to help pay for his trip. To repay the loan, he plans to pay her $16 each month from the money he earns at his part-time job. How much money will Lucas owe his mother after two months of payments?

_____

5 Although the number of students going on the eighth-grade trip has been decreasing at an average rate of 6 students per year for the last five years, the overall class size has stayed about 120 students. For each of the next five years, the school board projects an average increase of about 10% per year in the number of students in eighth grade. How might an increase in the number of eighth graders affect the decreasing number of students going on the class trip? Explain your answer on the back of this page.

52

Name _____   Date _____

It's in the Cards

Integers Review

Tom likes to play card games. He created a game that uses a standard deck of cards but with the jacks, kings, queens, and jokers removed. The value of each card is the same as the number on the card's face, but aces are worth 20 points. Red cards are negative, and black cards are positive. (Hearts and diamonds are red; spades and clubs are black.) The score is tallied by adding the positive and negative values of the cards. Each person is dealt a hand of five cards. The person with the most points at the end of a game is the winner. Tom recently played a game with Evan, Sara, and Su Lee. The cards for the first hand are shown. Solve the following problems.

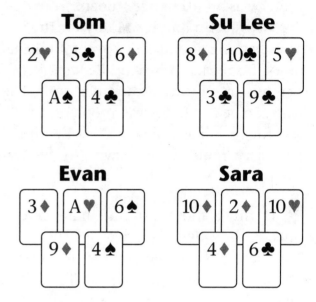

1 Find each person's score.

Tom _____   Evan _____

Sara _____   Su Lee _____

2 Arrange the players' scores from highest to lowest.

_____

What is the difference between the highest and lowest scores?

_____

What is the average score of all the players?

_____

3 At the start of the second game, Tom was dealt a great hand: the ace of spades, ace of clubs, 10 of spades, 2 of diamonds, and the 6 of hearts. What was his score?

_____

Tom felt that because he had three of the four highest-scoring cards, his score could not be beat. Find at least one hand that could beat his score.

_____

4 In the next game, Tom was dealt a hand of five red cards. What is the highest possible score he could have?

_____

What is the lowest possible score he could have?

_____

5 If Tom has three black cards and two red cards, he feels his score will be positive because there are more black cards than red ones. Do you agree? Explain your answer on the back of this page.

Practice, Practice, Practice! Word Problems   Scholastic Teaching Resources

53

Name _____   Date _____

Temperature Highs and Lows

Dieter was an exchange student from Germany who came to live with Justin and his family for the school year. The boys soon became good friends and found that they could learn much from each other. While Justin was familiar with temperatures on the Fahrenheit scale, Dieter used the Celsius scale. Solve the following problems involving temperature. Use the formulas $C = (F - 32) \div 1.8$ and $F = (C \times 1.8) + 32$. If necessary, round your answers to the nearest whole degree.

1 During a snowstorm, the boys were outside shoveling the driveway. Dieter remarked that the temperature must be about 10 degrees below zero. When Justin laughed and told him it was not that cold, the boys realized that Dieter was speaking of temperature on the Celsius scale. What is –10°C on the Fahrenheit scale?

_____

2 Justin told Dieter that in winter his family kept the thermostat at 68°F during the day and 55°F at night. What are these temperatures on the Celsius scale?

_____

3 Dieter told Justin that in summer his family kept the air-conditioning set at 25°C. Express this temperature in degrees Fahrenheit.

_____

4 One day Justin caught the flu and had a fever of 102°F. Convert this to degrees Celsius.

_____

The normal body temperature of a person is 98.6°F. What does this equal on the Celsius scale?

_____

5 In June, a few days before Dieter was to leave for home, Dieter noted that the Celsius thermometer he had read 35°. What was this temperature in degrees Fahrenheit?

_____

After a thunderstorm that evening, the temperature dropped to 28° Celsius. What was this temperature in degrees Fahrenheit?

_____

6 Compare and contrast the Fahrenheit and Celsius temperature scales. What might be an advantage measuring temperatures in degrees Celsius rather than degrees Fahrenheit? Explain.

_____

_____

_____

_____

Name _____ Date _____

Mail Call

Liz and her mother do a lot of their shopping through mail order catalogs. Solve the following problems that are based on their last order. If necessary, round your answers to the nearest cent.

1 Liz found a pair of jeans she liked. If she bought one pair at a price of $29.95, she could buy a second pair for half price. What was the total she would pay for the two pairs of jeans?

_____

2 There was a special on sweatshirts. Each sweatshirt was on sale for $9.69. If a customer bought three sweatshirts at the regular price of $12.95, a fourth sweatshirt was free. Which is the better buy? Four sweatshirts at $9.69 each or three sweatshirts at $12.95 and a fourth one free?

_____

3 The list price of a winter coat was $139.79, but the coat was discounted 25%. What was the cost of the coat?

_____

The list price of another winter coat was $149.99, but this coat was discounted by $\frac{1}{3}$. What was the cost of this coat?

_____

4 A sweater that was regularly priced at $35.95 was reduced to $26.96. What was the percent of decrease?

_____

5 Liz and her mother's order came to $157.69. They also had to pay a sales tax of 3.5% and a shipping and handling charge of $10.95. What was the total cost of their order?

_____

6 Liz and her mother like to comparison shop. Sneakers for $59.99 were marked off 25%. What was the cost of the sneakers?

_____

The same sneakers were for sale in a catalog for $35.99, but the shipping cost was $6.99. What was the cost of the sneakers?

_____

Which is the better buy?

_____

7 Even though they live near shopping malls, Liz and her mother choose to buy things by mail and over the Internet. What reasons might they have? Explain.

_____

_____

_____

_____

Practice, Practice, Practice! Word Problems   Scholastic Teaching Resources

55

Name _____   Date _____

Summer Pool Party

Amanda and her mother decided to have a pool party. Amanda invited 25 of her friends. She soon realized that a lot of planning and a lot of math were necessary to have a successful party. For each of the problems below, cross out information that is not needed, then solve the problem.

1 Amanda and her mother decided to buy 36 12-ounce bottles of spring water for $7.99, 24 12-ounce cans of cola for $5.99, and a dozen 8-ounce cans of fruit juice for $2.69. What was the total cost of the water, cola, and fruit juice?

_____

2 For snacks, Amanda bought three bags of potato chips for $2.49 each and three bags of pretzels. Each bag of pretzels weighed 18 ounces and cost $2.19. What was the total cost of the potato chips and pretzels?

_____

3 Amanda decided to buy three new CDs to add to the atmosphere of her party. The CDs were on sale and were discounted 20%. If Amanda bought two CDs at the discounted price of $15.99, she would get a third CD for half of the discounted price. What was the total cost of the CDs? (Round your answer to the nearest cent if necessary.)

_____

4 Amanda planned to conclude the pool party by offering her friends ice cream sundaes. She and her mother bought three $\frac{1}{2}$-gallon containers of chocolate and vanilla ice cream for $3.99 each. Each half gallon contained 16 servings of ice cream. They also bought three separate toppings (priced $1.99, $1.79, and $1.49) for a total of $5.27. Finally, they bought plastic cups, napkins, and spoons for $9.79. What was the total cost for the ice cream, toppings, plastic cups, napkins, and spoons?

_____

5 Before buying all of the items for the party, Amanda's mother estimated that the total cost would be about $23 more than what she would have liked to spend. What items could Amanda eliminate to stay within her mother's budget and still have enough for the party? Explain.

_____

_____

_____

_____

Practice, Practice, Practice! Word Problems   Scholastic Teaching Resources

Name _____ Date _____

"School Stats"

In Cassie's town, the school board publishes information about the local schools each year. The pamphlet, called "School Stats," has interesting information. Recently, when looking through it, Cassie learned much about the schools in her town. Solve the following problems. (If necessary, round your answers to the nearest whole number.)

1 Three-fourths of the high school's graduating class went on to college last year. The graduating class had 320 students. How many students went to college?

_____

2 In a recent poll, 60% of the middle school students preferred pizza for lunch on Friday, 27% preferred tacos, and 13% preferred hot dogs. The middle school has 860 students. For Friday lunches, how many preferred pizza?

_____

How many preferred tacos? _____

How many preferred hot dogs? _____

If $1\frac{3}{4}$ times as many preferred hot dogs to salad, how many preferred salad?

_____

3 Of 648 sixth and seventh graders, $\frac{2}{3}$ bring their lunch to school at least once each week. How many sixth and seventh graders bring their lunch at least once each week?

_____

4 3,280 students attend the town's schools. Sixty-five percent of the students walk to school on nice days. How many students walk to school on these days?

_____

On rainy or snowy days, the number of students walking to school is reduced by a fourth. How many students walk to school on rainy or snowy days?

_____

5 To reduce the overcrowding in the town's schools, the board of education has proposed building a new elementary school. Three separate polls were taken. In the first poll, 62% of 268 people supported the building of a new school. In the second poll, slightly more than half of 336 people supported the building of a new school. In the third poll, 38% of 92 people supported the building of a new school. Based on the polls, do you believe the general population of the town would support the building of a new school? Explain you answer on the back of this page.

Practice, Practice, Practice! Word Problems Scholastic Teaching Resources

Name _____ Date _____

Down by the Sea

Derrick and his family enjoy going to the beach during the summer. Between swimming and the amusements on the boardwalk, there is always plenty to do. Solve the following problems. If necessary, round your answers to the nearest cent.

1 Daily beach fees are $3.00 for adults and $1.50 for children ages 12 to 17. Children 11 and under are free. What was the total cost for daily beach passes for Derrick, who is 13 years old, his father, mother, 16-year-old sister, and 9-year-old brother?

_____

Season beach passes are $30.00 for adults and $15.00 for children ages 12 to 17. If Derrick's parents bought season passes for the family, how many times would the family have to go to the beach for the season passes to be a better buy than daily passes?

_____

2 After spending the day at the beach, Derrick and his family ate dinner on the boardwalk. The bill came to $35.65. Sales tax on the meal was 4.5%. What was the total cost for dinner?

_____

Derrick's father paid the bill with a $50 bill. How much change did he receive?

_____

If Derrick's father wanted to leave a 15% tip, based on the total bill, how much should he leave?

_____

3 After dinner, the family went to the amusement pier to go on rides. They had to buy tickets. The tickets came in books of 25 for $25.00, 50 for $45.00, and 100 for $90.00. What is the discount on the cost of books of 50 and 100 tickets compared to books of 25 tickets?

_____

4 The rides on the amusement pier require 3 to 5 tickets each. What is the fewest number of rides that can be taken if the family purchased a book of 25 tickets?

_____

What is the most number of rides that can be taken? _____

What is the fewest number of rides that can be taken on a book of 50 tickets?

_____

What is the most number of rides? _____

What is the fewest number of rides that can be taken on a book of 100 tickets?

_____

What is the most number of rides? _____

Answer Key

Body Facts, page 9

1. 144
2. 210; 3.5
3. 607
4. 1,200; 28,800
5. 4,167; 69
6. Answers may vary; a possible answer follows: He could choose 2 hamburgers with buns, 1 baked potato with butter, 1 glass of low-fat milk, and 1 small salad with dressing. Combined with the calories he has already consumed at breakfast and lunch, this will give him a total of 2,860 calories, 40 calories less than his upper limit of 2,900.

Highs and Lows, page 10

1. 6,201 feet
2. 7,391 feet
3. 65,233 feet; 12 miles
4. 16,480 feet; about 20 feet less
5. 15

Taryn's Fractions, page 11

1. $8\frac{1}{8}$ miles
2. $\frac{5}{6}$ quart
3. $\frac{3}{4}$ hour (45 minutes)
4. $13\frac{5}{6}$ miles
5. Taryn's; $\frac{3}{8}$ inch
6. Yes. Her estimates add up to $1\frac{1}{12}$, but this is a close approximation.

Harris Middle School, page 12

1. 18
2. 12
3. 18
4. 24; 48; 40; $\frac{3}{8}$
5. 18; $10\frac{1}{2}$ feet
6. No. The plan is not accurate because only 12 bulbs are left.

Dan's Ski Trip, page 13

1. $5\frac{1}{4}$ minutes
2. 5 miles
3. Dan; $\frac{1}{20}$ mile
4. 3; 8
5. $2\frac{3}{5}$ miles
6. Answers may vary; a possible answer follows: Yes. Dan rounded each distance to the nearest whole number and added them. Although he actually skied $10\frac{7}{8}$ miles, this is a close estimate.

Uncle Al's Bakery, page 14

1. 18
2. 16
3. $12\frac{3}{4}$
4. 5; $\frac{1}{3}$ of $2\frac{1}{4}$ cups or $\frac{3}{4}$ cup; $1\frac{1}{2}$ cups
5. 20
6. $10\frac{1}{2}$ cups of biscuit mix; $4\frac{1}{2}$ cups of secret ingredient
7. No. Since Uncle Al sold 21 dozen cookies, he had only 3 dozen left. He needed 4 dozen to fill the order.

Track Team Decimals, page 15

1. 5:15 P.M.
2. 8.5 hours
3. 0.36 second; 0.57 second
4. 1.26 seconds; 0.28 second
5. Darrin; 0.55 mile
6. Answers may vary; a possible answer follows: If Darrin continues to improve by an average of 0.21 second per week, he will improve his time from 13.25 to 13.04 in one more week. He has three more days after that to improve slightly more than 0.04 second. But he may not be able to do so because of physical limitations.

David and Decimals, page 16

1. 7.2 kilometers per hour
2. $7.30
3. $913
4. 42 inches; 3.5 feet
5. 52.2 miles per hour; 2.9 hours; 2 hours 54 minutes
6. David is correct. Neil divided 2.5 by 10 instead of dividing 10 by 2.5.

Weather Extremes, page 17

1. 265.47 inches; 41
2. 102.01 inches; 8.765 inches; 3 inches; 0.25 foot
3. 3.16 inches per hour
4. Heather was correct. If Christy averaged the four daily high temperatures, she would have gotten an average of 42.2°F (rounded off). If she had averaged all seven temperatures, the average high temperature would be 40.3°F.

Camp Challenge, page 18

1. 33.25°F
2. 17.55 kilometers long
3. 3.1 kilometers per hour
4. 5.25 feet; 15.85 feet; 2.65 feet
5. Answers may vary; a possible answer follows: Mathematically, his time is 29.5 seconds, but he would probably not be able to keep up this pace in a real race.

The Class Trip, page 19

1. $30.86
2. $130.85
3. $164.25
4. 123
5. $2.50; Answers may vary; a possible answer follows: If they charged $3 per ticket, they would need to sell only 220 tickets and make a profit of $210.

Tyrel, Inc., page 20

1. $1.43
2. $116.25; $523.90
3. 110.5 hours
4. $6.50
5. $640.04
6. $24.80
7. Tyrel earns more by being paid by the hour, $33.75, as opposed to $28.57 if he is paid a flat fee.

Lights Out!, page 21

1. $12.98; $7.02; 1 $5 bill, 2 $1 bills, 2 pennies
2. $23.14; $26.86; 1 $20 bill, 1 $5 bill, 1 $1 bill, 3 quarters, 1 dime, and 1 penny (Students might suggest 1 half-dollar and 1 quarter rather than 3 quarters.)
3. $21.42; $8.58; 1 $5 bill, 3 $1 bills, 2 quarters (or 1 half-dollar), 1 nickel, 3 pennies
4. This would allow Alvaro to give him a $10 bill for change.

Around Town, page 22

1. 3:4
2. 4:1; 5:1
3. 2:3; 10:1
4. 8:7; 15:7
5. 1:2; 1:4
6. Both are correct. Heather's ratio is in simplest form.

Aunt Sarah's Bookstore, page 23

1. 12; 4
2. 80; 120
3. 738
4. 168; 28
5. 107
6. No. The number of customers and the number of books they buy will vary throughout the day.

Numbers by Many Names, page 24

1. 260; 234; 351
2. Kerri, 80%; Roberto, 70%; Taylor and Cara, 75%
3. 24; 42
4. 494; 1,495
5. Yes. 25% is the same as $\frac{1}{4}$. Multiplying by $\frac{1}{4}$ is the same as dividing by 4.

The Class Picnic, page 25

1. 114
2. 156; 84
3. 30; 54; 27; 9
4. 13; 108
5. The numbers could not be correct because they add up to 104%.

Time for Hoops, page 26

1. 100%; 7
2. 15; 18
3. 112
4. 24; 203
5. 180
6. 44; 45; 20. Answers may vary; a possible answer follows: Trish is the best scorer because she made 40% of 110 field goal tries. Although Sienna made 50% of the field goals she attempted, she attempted only 40 field goals, which is not a lot over the course of a season. Had she taken more shots, it is quite possible her percentage of shots made would have gone down.

Play Ball!, page 27

1. 31%; 13%
2. 63%; 16%; 21%
3. 20%; 83%
4. 60%; 50%. No, because they may have had several hits in the same games and no hits in other games.

Reaching the Goal, page 28

1. $3,215; $1,929
2. 180; $5.14; $1,605; 50%
3. $220
4. $126; $93; exact answer is $12.74 but a more practical answer is $12.75
5. Answers may vary; a possible answer follows: No. Very few students participated in the candy sale. Had more participated, the fee for the dance could have been less.

A Special Promotion, page 29

1. 18%; 355
2. 28%; 68.3 = 68
3. 27%; 27%
4. $65; 15%; 8%
5. Answers may vary; a possible answer follows: Disagree. Since Krystal doesn't know how many hamburgers are usually sold, her conclusion is wrong.

Election Day, page 30

1. 102; 51; 34
2. 56%; 10%
3. 40%; 74%
4. Answers may vary; a possible answer follows: Kareem is probably correct. 52% of 92 students is 48 and 46% of 92 students is 42. This is not a wide gap. Since 44 students did not respond and 2% were undecided, it is possible that many of these votes could go to Alexis in the election.

Shopping at the Mall, page 31

1. $4.50; $25.49
2. $22.49; $67.46
3. $11.94; $27.85
4. $3.99; $15.96
5. $1.75; $33.24
6. $2.20; $19.75
7. The second store was less expensive, $21.24 compared to $21.37.

Moving to the Burbs, page 32

1. $69.25
2. $83.46
3. $19.84; $7.30
4. $60.56
5. $94.07; $0.63
6. Answers may vary; a possible answer follows: The cost in state would be $3,040.75 and the cost out of state would be $2,997.31. However, after the cost of gasoline for the 150-mile trip is added in, the overall savings is only about $30. This amount may not be worth a three-hour drive.

Cashing in Big, page 33

1. $1.88
2. $3.30; $13.20
3. $0.75
4. Kelli is wrong. Her account gained more interest only because she deposited more money. Her rate of interest is lower.

Time to Remodel, page 34

1. $94.40; $389.40
2. $238.74; $1,234.53
3. $94.42; $27
4. $427.56
5. Answers may vary; a possible answer follows: Cheryl is right. Although the interest rate at Jones Bank is lower, the term of the loan is a year longer. The interest for the loan at Smith bank is $1,600 and at Jones Bank it is $1,875.

A Fish Story, page 35

1. $52.42; $157.27; $162.77
2. $158.53
3. $94.99; $590.78
4. Answers may vary; a possible answer follows: The cost of the aquarium in the store is $79.14. Buying the same aquarium over the Internet, plus paying for shipping, will cost $77.46, resulting in a savings of $1.68. Most people would likely find this savings to be minimal and would buy the aquarium from the store.

Kim's Averages, page 36

1. 94.2
2. 81.4
3. 91.5; 89.8
4. 87; 88.5
5. Yes. Kim calculated Carl's average correctly by adding Carl's 5 test scores and then dividing by 5.

Running Out of Time, page 37

1. 8 hours 45 minutes; 45 minutes more; $\frac{3}{4}$ hour
2. 3 hours 35 minutes
3. 4:05 P.M.
4. 8 hours 15 minutes; $53.63
5. Answers may vary; a possible answer follows: No. There is not enough time, especially to do his research. He might be able to change his hours at the sandwich shop, go to the party later, or wake up earlier in the morning.

Down on the Farm, page 38

1. 33 pounds 4 ounces
2. 12
3. 16 feet 5 inches
4. 165
5. 8; $\frac{1}{2}$ pint
6. The area is 72 square yards. This should be multiplied by 9, because 1 square yard is equal to 9 square feet. Kirsten's father should buy enough seed to cover 648 square feet.

Think Metric, page 39

1. 3.5 meters; 3; 1.15 meters
2. 320 grams; 0.32
3. 84 kilometers per hour
4. 640-gram box; six-pack; 0.13 liter
5. Answers may vary; a possible answer follows: Based on multiples of 10, the metric system is easier to use.

Moving In, page 40

1. $\frac{1}{4}$ hour or 15 minutes
2. 4 hours 55 minutes
3. 0.35 meter; 35 centimeters
4. 10$\frac{2}{3}$ yards; 32 feet
5. yes; 2 cups
6. No. The plants will be too heavy by 0.58 kilogram.

Lori the Landscaper, page 41

1. 384 feet; 48; $767.52
2. 6,272 square feet; 224 square feet; 6,048 square feet; 2,016 square feet; 8,064 square feet
3. 192 square feet; 576 flowers; 56 feet

Carissa's Circles, page 42

1. 78.5 square feet; 31.4 feet
2. 200.96 square feet; 75.36 feet
3. 254.34 square inches; 56.52 inches; 197.82 square inches; 75.36 inches
4. Answers may vary; a possible answer follows: The rectangular bed has an area of 1,152 square inches. The circular bed has an area of 907.46 square feet and might be too small.

Moving Out, page 43

1. 600 cubic feet; 1,800 cubic feet
2. 12; 16
3. 2,520 cubic inches; 1,680 cubic inches
4. 600 cubic inches
5. Genaro was incorrect. The volume of the small box is 2 cubic feet. The volume of the large box is 16 cubic feet.

Packing Up, page 44

1. 31.5 square feet
2. 212 square inches; yes; 364 square inches
3. 112 square inches; 376 square inches
4. 750 square feet; 2 gallons
5. No. The first box has a surface area of 62 square inches. The second box has a surface area of 82 square inches.

James and Geometry, page 45

1. 252 square feet; 464.75 square feet
2. 60,480 cubic inches; 261.82 gallons
3. 19.63 square feet; 15.7 feet
4. 180 feet
5. 46 square feet
6. He is correct. They could place 12 tiles down and 12 across to cover 64 square feet.

Surf's Up!, page 46

1. June; 25
2. February; 2
3. February–March, March–April, April–May
4. July–August, August–September, September–October
5. 22; 15; 7
6. June and July
7. winter
8. Answers may vary; a possible answer follows: The sales of surfboards increase from February to June. Sales decrease from June to November, then increase slightly for December. Sales increase in anticipation of summer and the December gift-giving season.

Time for Lunch, page 47

1. hot dog; 38; pizza; 32
2. tuna sandwich; 7; ham sandwich; 14
3. 14; 13
4. 34%; 34%; 19%
5. Answers may vary; a possible answer follows: Hamburgers are preferred by only 38 students, and the tuna sandwich is preferred by only 23 students.

A Piece of the Pie, page 48

1. 25%; $610
2. 9%; $219.60
3. $390.40
4. $414.80; $170.80
5. $97.60
6. Answers may vary; a possible answer follows: Yes, but if they have two dances and two flea markets, it is possible that attendance, and potential profits, at the events may go down.

Picture This, page 49

1. 3
2. Wallace
3. 33
4. 30
5. 18
6. McDermott and Wallace
7. Answers may vary; a possible answer follows: Yes. It is valid, because averages can be misleading. What is needed is a breakdown of each class and the number of students it contains.

The Chances Are . . . , page 50

1. $\frac{1}{36}$; $\frac{1}{18}$; $\frac{1}{12}$
2. $\frac{1}{25}$; $\frac{1}{5}$; $\frac{1}{5}$
3. $\frac{1}{12}$; $\frac{1}{6}$
4. No. In this case, some skill is involved, making the probability of each event unequal.

Scoring with Integers, page 51

1. −6; Falcons' 14-yard line
2. 29
3. 32; 4
4. 13
5. Yes. They gained a total of 50 yards, which would reach the goal line for a touchdown.

Class Trip to Disney World!, page 52

1. −30; 4 more years
2. +35; $215
3. −$24
4. $48
5. Answers may vary; a possible answer follows: An increase in students could result in more students going on the trip. This could offset the effect of the declining numbers.

It's in the Cards, page 53

1. Tom: 21; Evan: −22; Sara: −20; Su Lee: 9
2. Tom, Su Lee, Sara, Evan; 43; −3
3. 42; 10 of clubs, 9 of spades, 9 of clubs, 8 of spades, 8 of clubs
4. −14; −69
5. Answers may vary; a possible answer follows: Disagree, because his score depends on the value of the cards.

Temperature Highs and Lows, page 54

1. 14°F
2. 20°C; 13°C
3. 77°F
4. 39°C; 37°C
5. 95°F; 82°F
6. Answers may vary; a possible answer follows: Celsius, once learned, is easier to use because it has a range of 100° between the freezing and boiling points of water.

Mail Call, page 55

1. $44.93
2. 4 sweatshirts for $9.69 each
3. $104.84; $99.99
4. 25%
5. $174.16
6. $44.99; $42.98; catalog
7. Answers may vary; a possible answer follows: Some people prefer the convenience. Sometimes the prices may be lower.

Summer Pool Party, page 56

1. $16.67
2. $14.04
3. $39.98
4. $27.03
5. Answers may vary; a possible answer follows: Do not purchase the CDs and instead use ones she already has or borrow CDs from friends.

"School Stats," page 57

1. 240
2. 516; 232; 112; 64
3. 432
4. 2,132; 1,599
5. Answers may vary; a possible answer follows: No. The overall number of people polled is too small. Also, the results of the three polls vary.

Down by the Sea, page 58

1. $9; 11
2. $37.25; $12.75; $5.59
3. 10%
4. 5; 8; 10; 16; 20; 33

Notes

Notes